C000278887

WORLD CUP
MOMENTS

Published by Times Books
An imprint of HarperCollins Publishers
Westerhill Road, Bishopbriggs, Glasgow G64 2QT
www.harpercollins.co.uk

HarperCollins Publishers
1st Floor, Watermarque Building, Ringsend Road, Dublin 4, Ireland

First edition 2022

© Times Newspapers Ltd 2022

The Times® is a registered trademark of Times Newspapers Ltd

All rights reserved. No part of this publication may be reproduced, stored in a retrieval system,
or transmitted, in any form or by any means, electronic, mechanical, photocopying, recording
or otherwise without the prior permission in writing of the publisher and copyright owners.

The contents of this publication are believed correct at the time of printing.
Nevertheless the publisher can accept no responsibility for errors or omissions,
changes in the detail given or for any expense or loss thereby caused.

A catalogue record for this book is available from the British Library

Thanks and acknowledgements go to Robin Ashton and
Joanne Lovey at News Syndication and, in particular,
at The Times, Ian Brunskill and, at HarperCollins,
Robin Scrimgeour, Harley Griffiths,
Jethro Lennox and Kevin Robbins.

ISBN 978-0-00-854784-4

10 9 8 7 6 5 4 3 2 1

Printed in Italy

If you would like to comment on any aspect of this book,
please contact us at the above address or online.
e-mail: times.books@harpercollins.co.uk

www.timesbooks.co.uk

This book is produced from independently certified FSC™ paper
to ensure responsible forest management.

For more information visit: www.harpercollins.co.uk/green

THE TIMES

WORLD CUP
MOMENTS

Richard Whitehead

Jules Rimet still gleaming: hat-trick hero Geoff Hurst and captain Bobby Moore parade the World Cup to an ecstatic Wembley crowd. Nobby Stiles, right, joins in the fun.

Contents

Foreword

By Henry Winter
Chief Football Writer, *The Times*

World Cups are a celebration of the sport, a test of the human spirit and sinew, and in a strange, uplifting way a bringing together of nations by pitting them against each other.

World Cups are about the headers of a leaping Pelé for Brazil against Italy in 1970 and a flying Dutchman, Robin van Persie, against Spain in 2014. These special events that showcase and stress-test technique are also about the unforgettable volleys of David Platt for England against Belgium at Italia 90, and Argentina's Maxi Rodriguez against Mexico in 2006.

They're about the memorable dribbles of Diego Maradona against England in 1986 and, personally, also the privilege of being present to chronicle Saudi Arabia's Saeed Al-Owairan slaloming through half of Belgium in a sweltering Washington in 1994 and Michael Owen slicing through Argentina in St Étienne at France 98. The memories of those goals, of the breath being taken away, never leaves you.

World Cups are about seismic upsets, results that shook the world, like the USA defeating mighty England in 1950 and North Korea stunning Italy in 1966. They can concrete over Ayresome Park but they can never bury the legend of Pak Doo Ik's goal.

World Cups are about the geniuses in the dugout, about Louis van Gaal having the nerve and the nous to take off Jasper Cillessen for Tim Krul for the Netherlands' penalty shoot-out against Costa Rica in 2014. Krul saved the day, stopping two penalties, and the Dutch, almost nonchalantly, put both Cillessen and Krul up for interview the next day in Rio.

I was en route to Brazil's training ground up in the hills when I heard the pair were to speak. I jumped out at the lights on the way out of Rio, although it was more a gentle hop given the stuttering traffic. I hailed a cab going back into town, reaching the Dutch retreat, at a stadium belonging to Flamengo, to catch Cillessen and Krul sitting side by side, speaking without a care in the world.

Cillessen very calmly accepted Van Gaal's decision, understanding it was for the good of the team. The World Cup is about stories, sporting ones, human interest ones, lessons in life.

Every time I return from a World Cup, and Qatar will be my ninth, a week's decompression is de rigueur because the tournament is so wonderfully intense – and I'm only reporting. I'm not physically or emotionally engaged like the players reaching out for the greatest prize in sport or riding the supporters' rollercoaster. It is impossible not to get swept up in a World Cup. It's so stirring, even after repeated visits. It's the sight of opposing fans making friends, an example to their political leaders. It's the sound of tens of thousands of Chilean fans singing on Copacabana Beach at 4am in 2014. We weren't wanting to sleep, honestly.

It's the England followers celebrating Gareth Southgate in 2018, sending waistcoat sales soaring. It's the unbelievable hordes of Argentina fans in No 10 shirts, sending pulses racing simply at the thought of Maradona or Lionel Messi. It's the classic shirts; Argentina, Italy and Brazil. And Peru, simply for the legend Teófilo Cubillas in that beautiful white top with a red sash.

My first World Cup was Italia 90, not a classic technical tournament, but I still got to see Maradona open up Brazil's defence with a right-footed pass, off-balance, through for Claudio Caniggia to slide the ball past Cláudio Taffarel. Brazil then seemed to spend the rest of the game in Turin attempting to kick anyone

Argentinian. Those memories remain eternal, as does the recollection of the kindly Italian couple patiently explaining the ticketing system on the Turin tram on the way to Stadio Delle Alpi. We were almost there by the time I understood. Such moments help shape an individual's perception of a country.

World Cups bequeath a legacy of impressions: Ronaldo gaining redemption in 2002 for his faint and failure four years earlier, Brazilian fans saluting the rampant Germans through their tears in 2014, and Kylian Mbappe lighting up Moscow four years later. World Cups are so much more than what happens in the stadiums. It's being on the Champs-Élysées for the mother, father and extended family of all parties after France won the World Cup in 1998. It's the lady running my small hotel near the Coliseum in Rome insisting on washing and pressing all my shirts so I looked smart when returning home; the kindness of strangers.

It's also the insight into supreme professionals. It's the sight of the Colombian singer Shakira diligently doing her sound test the day before the 2006 final in Berlin. A storm whipped in, sparks tripped off the cables, and Shakira just carried on regardless, totally professional, leaving nothing to chance, no stray notes, nothing. Her performance the following day at the global showpiece was perfection.

So enjoy how *The Times* reported the moments from the ages. I wanted to become a football writer after reading Geoffrey Green's match reports in *The Times* because they captured the importance of the occasion, the drama of the game, but also told me about the setting, the country, the noises off. World Cups are so much more than about the sport and *The Times World Cup Moments* reflects that.

Introduction

By Richard Whitehead

To spend a few hours immersed in the archives of *The Times* – which begin on the impossibly far-off date of January 1 1785 – is to walk down the corridors of history, stopping off at whatever moment you choose to read how events that shaped the world were first reported. Wars, assassinations, political upheavals, technological revolutions, cultural revolutions – they are all there.

And so, naturally, are more trivial matters that nevertheless hold a deep significance and resonance for millions. Sport features high in this category. In *The Times* you can read about WG Grace, Don Bradman or Shane Warne. About Fred Perry, Rod Laver or Roger Federer. Or take your pick of Bobby Jones, Jack Nicklaus or Tiger Woods. In football, you'll find Steve Bloomer and Billy Meredith, Stanley Matthews and Garrincha, Pelé and George Best, Diego Maradona and Lionel Messi. In thousands of pages of digitised newsprint, you can locate them all, and hundreds more.

In this book are assembled many of the highlights of more than 70 years of coverage of the World Cup – the greatest event in the most popular sport on Earth – selected from the pages of *The Times*. In every part of the globe where football is followed with religious fervour, these moments and memories will chime with millions.

Stop a by-passer on the streets of Rio de Janeiro, for instance, and you could discuss the golden team of 1970, or their doomed heirs of 1982. Just don't mention the 7-1 semi-final humiliation by Germany in 2014. In Buenos Aires, you could end up debating the merits of Maradona in 1986 against Mario Kempes in 1978. Parisians might contend that the French World Cup winners of 1998, who triumphed on home soil, hold a greater place in national affections than those in 2018. In Germany, the narrative that sport is of limited wider significance is challenged by memories of an unexpected victory in the final in 1954, an event that is thought to have been a crucial factor in triggering the resurgence of the nation.

And the English are blessed and burdened with a whole range of sweet and sour World Cup memories – encompassing the triumph of 1966, the shattered hopes of 2018, the trauma of numerous penalty shoot-out defeats and the red cards shown to star players at key moments in knockout games.

This book contains most of the moments you would expect – the startling emergence of the 17-year-old Pelé in 1958, Geoff Hurst's disputed goal in the final of 1966, both of Maradona's goals (the ridiculous and the sublime) for Argentina against England in 1986, Paul Gascoigne's tears in Turin, the sound of vuvuzelas welcoming the World Cup to Africa in 2010, the battles in Berne in 1954 and Santiago in 1962. But there are also many you might not expect – or perhaps had just forgotten about.

Unearthing and selecting them has been a joy, but it has also been a revealing journey through the changing nature of the newspaper's coverage of football in general and the World Cup in particular. In 1930, for instance, when the first tournament was held in Uruguay, *The Times* provided no coverage at all for its readers. It was not alone in this lofty indifference: The *Daily Telegraph* and the *Daily Express* did not mention the tournament either. This had much to do with the fact that the FA had shown no interest in sending the England team to compete. In fact it was not until the climax of the third competition in France in 1938 that *The Times* acknowledged the World Cup's existence with a filler paragraph from the Reuters agency on Monday June 20 announcing that Italy had retained the "World Association Football Cup" by beating Hungary 4-2 in Paris.

The situation changed only gradually. In 1950, when the home nations entered for the first time and England were one of the 13 teams taking part, full match reports were published, though these came from Reuters. Geoffrey Green, the renowned football correspondent, covered his first World Cup in Switzerland in 1954, decorating the grey, austere pages with his flights of literary fancy, and was also in attendance in Sweden in 1958, though he did not travel to Chile in 1962.

For the 1966 competition in England, the paper mounted its biggest operation yet. Green was joined in reporting on the matches – and in those days match reports were still pretty much the only coverage – by two writers who later became better known as TV commentators, Barry Davies and Gerald Sinstadt, as well as Tony Pawson, a county cricketer and world fly-fishing champion who had played briefly for Charlton Athletic. Not that these names were visible to the public – *The Times* did not introduce bylines for its journalists until January 1967.

What would now be recognised as modern coverage of the competition began to emerge in 1990 where the paper had four writers in Italy and employed Graham Taylor, about to take over as England manager, as a columnist. By the French World Cup eight years later those numbers, and the amount of space devoted to the tournament, had increased enormously. And there was one significant change that pointed forwards into the 21st century: under the masthead on the front page was now the address of the *Times'* website.

Now, the competition is given blanket coverage across the organisation's multiple platforms – the printed newspaper, the website and the app. Match reports and photographs appear as quickly as possible after the final whistle in digital formats, reporters record video interviews and engage with comments from readers at the end of their articles, podcasts are produced every day – light years away from the leisurely wait for the paper to arrive at the next morning's breakfast table.

In most cases, these extracts are presented exactly as they appeared in *The Times* (and, on a few occasions, *The Sunday Times*), although sometimes there have been minor edits and changes have been made to reflect more modern styles. And new words have been written when – for a variety of reasons – the moments were not reported at sufficient length or depth at the time.

It is a glorious collection, showcasing the talents of some of the greatest writers in the history of football, presented alongside many stunning photographs. Here is a different version of the history of the world.

THE WORLD'S CUP

Enter the champions

Uruguay 4 Romania 0

21 July 1930 | Montevideo
Group 3

In truth, their entry to the pitch at the newly completed Estadio Centenario looks a little precarious. Uruguay, the hosts and overwhelming favourites, are emerging for their second group match against Romania, and the path to the playing area seems to be over an unsteady builders' walkway, covering what looks like a trench. But there was no need for concern – once on the turf the Uruguayans operated with sure-footed certainty: they won 4-0 to secure a semi-final against Yugoslavia. In the last four, they scored another six goals before meeting sterner opposition in the shape of bitter South American rivals Argentina. There they recovered from the shock of falling 2-1 behind before half-time to run out 4-2 winners. They received the trophy from FIFA's French president Jules Rimet, whose ambitious concept the global tournament had been. The first World Cup was several light years from the modern tournaments that seem to stop the globe spinning on its axis. Just 13 nations entered and only four European teams made the sea crossing to Uruguay. The British were not even members of FIFA and the UK media studiously ignored the competition. Still, Uruguay could lay justifiable claim to being the best team in the world – they had already underlined their credentials by winning the Olympic tournaments of 1924 and 1928.

RICHARD WHITEHEAD

Uruguay are led out by strongman captain José Nasazzi, nicknamed "the great marshal", followed by José Leandro Andrade, football's first black superstar, left-back Ernesto Mascheroni, and goalkeeper Enrique Ballesteros.

England's first flying visit

England head off into the unknown

19 June 1950 | London Airport

It may have been the fourth tournament, but as far as England were concerned the World Cup story began at what was then still usually called 'London' Airport on a Tuesday in June 1950. *The Times* sent a photographer to record the majority of the squad boarding a Pan-American Constellation for Flight 261 to Rio de Janeiro, and published an image on the picture page at the back of the newspaper. But it played second fiddle to 'Wild Irises on the Isle of Wight' and two photos of a camp in North Malaya to retrain Chinese communists. The sports desk ignored the squad's departure completely, displaying the haughty indifference to the competition which had led to the FA refusing to enter the previous tournaments. Football Correspondent Geoffrey Green was not dispatched to cover the World Cup, the paper instead published match reports from the Reuters agency, but there were eight journalists from English newspapers on board (as well as four English referees). Manager Walter Winterbottom was moderately bullish. "Our men have the ability and I feel that if they strike the form they showed in Belgium and have a fair amount of good fortune they are bound to do well," he said. His optimism was misplaced – after being humiliated by the United States and beaten by Spain, they failed to qualify from their group and were soon heading home again.

RICHARD WHITEHEAD

The majority of the England squad pose for the cameras before leaving for their ill-starred World Cup debut in Brazil. Manager Walter Winterbottom and captain Billy Wright used the microphone for short speeches for the newsreels.

Introducing Pelé

Brazil 5 Sweden 2

29 June 1958 | Stockholm
Final

FROM GEOFFREY GREEN,
ASSOCIATION FOOTBALL CORRESPONDENT

Brazil came to life that moment at the ninth minute when Garrincha, receiving from Didi, left Axbom stranded, swept into the by-line for Vavá to flash in his diagonal cross. That was 1-1 and a moment later Pelé nearly uprooted the Swedish post with a left foot shot from 20 yards. But there was no holding Garrincha and again, at the half-hour it was the old echo – Pelé, Didi, Garrincha, the flick, the by-line, the diagonal cross, and Vavá striking again at close range. Ten minutes after the change of ends, Pelé with sleight of foot jugglery, flicked up a cross from Zagallo, balanced the ball on his instep, chipped it over Gustavsson and leapt round the centre-half to volley home. Who can live with this sort of stuff? That was 3-1 to Brazil and the signal for individual exhibition in all corners of the field.

Vavá and Pelé embrace after the former had given Brazil the lead in the final against Sweden.

Dogged pursuit unearths stolen trophy

England lose the World Cup

20 March 1966
Central Hall, Westminster

The World Cup, of solid gold and insured for £30,000, was stolen from a display cabinet in Central Hall, Westminster, yesterday. Engraved with a symbolic winged figure, it was on display as part of a stamp exhibition. The trophy, 12in tall and weighing 9lb, vanished while a Methodist service was being held in another part of the hall. Security guards noticed it at 11 o'clock.

An inner door of the exhibition room had been forced. The thief or thieves had removed a small padlock at the back of the glass-fronted cabinet. [...]

Present holders are Brazil. It was to be awarded in the world Association football contest, the final stages of which are to be played in England in July.

28 March

The World Cup was found last night by a man taking his dog for a walk in Beulah Hill, Norwood, South London.

It was lying, wrapped in newspapers, in the gateway leading to a large rambling three-storey house, surrounded on three sides by a garden.

The cup was taken to Cannon Row Police Station, where Mr Harold Mayes, publicity officer of the Football Association World Cup Organisation, identified it. It was undamaged.

It was Mr David Corbett, aged 26, a Thames lighterman, who found the cup. He said: "I was about to put the lead on Pickles, my mongrel dog, when I noticed he was sniffing at something near the path. I looked down and saw a bundle. I picked it up and saw it was wrapped in newspaper.

"I tore the bottom off and saw a black base. I tore the top off and saw gold and the words 'Brazil 1962'. I took it back indoors to show my wife. I couldn't believe it for a few minutes, then I got into the car and took it to the police. Pickles saw it first – he found it, the little darling."

Pickles basks in the limelight with his owners David and Jeannie Corbett.

Geoff Hurst's line in history

England 4 West Germany 2

30 July 1966
Wembley Stadium, London | Final

BY BRIAN GLANVILLE,
SUNDAY TIMES FOOTBALL CORRESPONDENT

Then, with 100 minutes gone, justice was belatedly done; England scored again. Stiles's fine, long, pass to the right put Ball totally clear. From somewhere or other, that remarkable little man, more sprite than footballer, found the energy for yet another burst. His centre on the run was perfectly executed. Hurst met it with a thundering right foot shot which left Tilkowski helpless as a statue. The ball hit the under side of the bar and came down – surely over the line?

Yet after that iniquitous German goal all was possible and we waited for interminable seconds, died a thousand deaths, while little Herr Dienst trotted over to his Russian linesman. The linesman gestured obscurely but dramatically – was he giving a goal, or indicating that the ball had bounced on the line? And then, at last, we saw Herr Dienst pointing to the middle. England, once more, were ahead.

Hurst watches from a prone position as his shot beats West Germany goalkeeper Hans Tilkowski, hits the bar and bounces down.

Moore accused on the road to Mexico

England captain arrested

25 May 1970

Bogotá

Bobby Moore, captain of the England World Cup football team, was ordered to appear before a court here tonight accused of taking a gold bracelet from a local jeweller's shop.

He was ordered not to leave Bogotá and stayed behind here when other England players left for Mexico City. The England squad had flown in earlier from Quito, Ecuador where they played yesterday.

British Embassy officials said the owner of the shop had filed charges against the player.

28 May

BY OUR FOREIGN STAFF

Bobby Moore, the England football captain who was conditionally released in Bogotá, Colombia, yesterday after an inquiry into allegations that he stole a £600 bracelet from a jewellery shop, flew to Mexico last night to join the rest of England's World Cup team.

Mr. Moore's release was announced by Judge Pedro Dorado who has been investigating the allegations. He said that he did not have enough evidence "at the moment to justify a charge of theft against Mr Moore". He said that Mr Moore would have to report to the Colombian consul in Mexico City as one of the conditions of his release. He would be fined £12 if he failed to do so.

The judge has 30 days to complete his report and hand it over to another judge, who will decide whether to commit Mr Moore to trial or free him unconditionally.

Mr Moore read a statement to newspaper men at the British Embassy in Bogotá in which he said that he was "very pleased and happy to be a free man once again and I am pleased that the accusations which have been made against me have been shown to be unfounded.

"Now all I want to do is to forget the incident and return to my job of playing football and help England retain the World Cup."

A cheerful wave from Bobby Moore as he touches down on Mexican soil, ready for the defence of the World Cup.

Banks of England proves best for saving

Brazil 1 England 0

7 June 1970 | Guadalajara
Group 3

Bobby Charlton had no doubts. "The greatest act of goalkeeping the world has ever seen," he said in a *Times* piece looking back on the Guadalajara epic before the two countries crossed swords again in the quarter-final of the 2002 World Cup. Pelé agreed: "It was a phenomenal save, the save of that tournament and most other tournaments you could care to mention." The moment that would go down in the mythology of the competition came after 18 minutes of a Brazil-England showdown that pitted the World Cup favourites against the holders. Carlos Alberto curled a delicious pass inside full-back Terry Cooper, and winger Jairzinho raced to the byline before crossing to where Pelé, 10 yards out, leapt to make a textbook downward header that sent the ball arrowing towards the bottom corner of the net, just inside Banks's right-hand post. First, the England goalkeeper had to move across from the other side of his goal, then dive down towards the ball, somehow anticipating its fiendish bounce just inside the six-yard area. He got his hand to it but still wasn't sure he had done enough. "Honest to God I thought it was a goal," he said. But his solid contact somehow sent the ball spinning upwards and over the bar, to the obvious astonishment of his captain Bobby Moore. "An effort of extraordinary ability," said Pelé.

RICHARD WHITEHEAD

His body twisted as he falls, Gordon Banks somehow keeps Pelé's header out of the net and over the bar.

Scotland's shambles in Argentina

Inquest on an ill-starred campaign

13 June 1978 | Mendoza

FROM NORMAN FOX, FOOTBALL CORRESPONDENT

During the few minutes in which Scotland were within a single well-aimed kick or master tactical stroke of an incredible revival here yesterday, the world at large was in a forgiving mood. But Scottish football cannot afford to feel entitled to comfort itself with the luxury of believing that the 1978 World Cup was another case of having a team of world beaters who were misled into two dreadful performances that one magnificent victory over the Netherlands could relegate to the back of the mind.

Alistair MacLeod is bound to be blamed for the overall performance and without doubt he came here more as a cheerleader than team manager. He has won little respect among his international colleagues, all of whom began this World Cup with more experience, and he made basic errors in selection that set the team unnecessary problems from the outset. His attitude of "let the opposition worry about us" was typical of a certain school of thinking that has too many followers in Britain. Few who act upon such a flimsy theory find more than limited success. At least Mr MacLeod has now admitted that he probably did have a lot to learn in "global terms."

Ally MacLeod responds to the media in a TV interview during Scotland's disastrous World Cup campaign in Argentina.

Gazza's tears touch the heart of a nation

England 1 West Germany 1

(West Germany win 4-3
on penalties)
4 July 1990 | Turin | Semi-final

It was ten minutes into extra time in England's titanic Italia 90 semi-final against West Germany that an incident occurred that – many believe – helped to change the face of English football forever. Throughout England's sometimes stuttering progress to the last four, the creative hub of the team had been the 23-year-old midfield player Paul Gascoigne. Before the tournament there had been doubts about his temperament – "daft as a brush," manager Bobby Robson famously called him – but he had grown in stature in each game. However, with the score at 1-1 in the midst of intense semi-final combat, for once his touch deserted him when he received the ball on the halfway line and, as he struggled to regain possession in a tussle with Thomas Berthold, he instinctively stretched out and mistimed a challenge that left Berthold writhing theatrically on the floor. Referee José Roberto Wright reached instantly for his yellow card: it was Gascoigne's second booking of the competition and meant he would miss the final if England went on to win. Millions watching on television saw Gascoigne's bottom lip quiver and tears well up in his eyes. Gary Lineker was seen gesturing to the bench to keep a close eye on his wellbeing in the next few minutes. In the stadium and the press box the tears went unseen – *Times* correspondent Stuart Jones did not mention them in his match report – but their significance went well beyond that moment. After years of decline into something approaching pariah status, the game in England began to regain a measure of respectability again at Italia 90. And, quite unwittingly, Paul Gascoigne – Gazza as he was always known – played a significant part in that gradual but ultimately astonishing rebirth.

RICHARD WHITEHEAD

A still-distraught Paul Gascoigne thanks the England supporters after a heartbreaking defeat on penalties in the semi-final.

Murder on the streets of Medellín

United States 2 Colombia 1

22 June 1994 | Los Angeles
Group A

4 July

FROM ROB HUGHES, FOOTBALL CORRESPONDENT

Colombia, though exotically gifted with individual talents, had, in the words of Francisco Maturana, their coach, "come to the party but failed to dance".

Quite why, he could not, or would not, say. He had led his side to an astonishing 5-0 World Cup qualifying victory against Argentina in Buenos Aires barely nine months previously; yet now, dubious to say the least, the Colombians acquiesced so neatly in their downfall to the United States that all manner of sinister questioning was thrown at Maturana.

He could explain nothing. Whether the lethargy, the strange lack of joy in a team noted for it, was due to a death threat that removed Gomez, the midfield player, from even the substitutes' bench two hours before the game, the coach could not confirm.

And he did not offer anything approaching an explanation as to why his side, so visibly gifted in movement and flair, had collapsed in morale.

I have never seen a side such as Colombia lie down to defeat in such a manner. [...]

But what the States were shy of fulfilling, Colombia contrived to do for them. Harkes, of Derby County, burst powerfully down the left wing, shooting once again without accuracy, but Escobar, the hapless defender, stretched and placed the ball firmly past Cordoba, his stranded goalkeeper, for the most blatant of own goals.

Andres Escobar, centre wearing No.2, sparks celebrations among the US players and fans after scoring an infamous own goal in Colombia's unexpected defeat by the United States.

FROM ROB HUGHES, FOOTBALL CORRESPONDENT

The struggle for football's soul and sanity goes on. Yesterday in Medellín, approaching 100,000 shocked citizens filed past the body of Andres Escobar, the unfortunate player whose own-goal against the United States helped to eliminate his country, Colombia, from the World Cup. In the first round of the competition, 91 goals were scored; one was an own-goal, and for that, it seems, Escobar was shot 12 times by his assailants outside the El Indio restaurant in Medellín. "Thanks for the auto-goal" were the last words he is said to have heard. [...]

Colombia is a place where life has always seemed more precarious than in many other parts. But its players, very gifted individuals, had arrived at this World Cup pledging their efforts "to show the world that our country is about more joyful things than drugs and murder".

Yet Colombia's defeat and humiliation by the United States, which was a brilliant result for conspiracy theorists, left a bitter taste, with huge disappointment that a team of such a high level of skill could perform so poorly.

Exit Maradona after failed drugs test

29 June 1994 | Dallas

FROM ROB HUGHES, FOOTBALL CORRESPONDENT

The return of Diego Armando Maradona was too good to be true, too bad to be condoned. The positive drugs test that betrayed him as the user of stimulants came after Argentina's second game of the World Cup, against Nigeria, but there had been a moment in the first, against Greece, that unnerved everybody who had followed his 90-match international career.

It was when Maradona produced a flicker of his old flame, when he found space with movement of his body that defies others to emulate or stop him, and then hit the ball into the net with his left foot with power and precision that was totally unforgiving. He then turned, ran towards the television cameras, and there was an intensity in the eyes that was almost demonic; the mouth was shouting incoherently, a vein was standing up in the neck.

Could this simply be the pent-up rage of a man whom so many had doubted? It seemed unlikely, one thought, even then, that there may be something more sinister, something in the chemical make-up of a man with convictions for drug abuse.

How could we explain to the children, to the future generation, that this was the finest and also one of the most corrupt footballers of his or any other lifetime? Maradona was simply the best, and the worst, performer of his time. Beauty laced with poison, genius flawed by greed.

FROM DAVID MILLER

The final indignity this week in a chequered career is enough to make you weep. Maradona has been destroyed as much by villainous treatment on the field over 15 years, and by media hounding, as by his own weaknesses. It is wretched how the public are too unforgiving and sanctimonious towards fallen sporting heroes when we accept without challenge the idiosyncrasies and psychological failures of the tortured genius in art, science, music or literature, such as Gauguin, Mendel, Elgar or Ibsen.

Diego Maradona faces the full fury of the world's press in Dallas after failing a drugs test, bringing the curtain down on his extraordinary World Cup career.

David Beckham realises the full impact of his actions as referee Kim Milton Nielsen raises his red card.

David Beckham – from hero to scapegoat

Argentina 2 England 2

(Argentina win 4-3 on penalties)
30 June 1998 | St Étienne |
Second round

FROM OLIVER HOLT, FOOTBALL CORRESPONDENT

The sad, shameful fact amid all the horrible, heartbreaking melodrama, though, is that England would surely have won this match were it not for the stupidity of Beckham. Just as the Manchester United pin-up boy had earned his rehabilitation at the heart of the England side, so he ruined it all with a moment of recklessness that left him far more culpable in this defeat than [David] Batty will ever be.

His trials and tribulations and his glorious return dominated this truncated campaign, but ultimately he betrayed himself with the lack of discipline that had made Glenn Hoddle, the England coach, wary of trusting him in the first place. A flick of his leg at [Diego] Simeone, the Argentina captain, after an innocuous foul early in the second half was enough to have him sent back to the dressing room and to change the course of the game.

"What he did cost us dearly," Hoddle said. [...]

Beckham, waiting to receive a pass near the centre circle, was fouled clumsily by Simeone. A free kick was awarded, but as Beckham lay on the floor he flicked his right leg up at Simeone and caught him on the calf. It was right under the nose of Kim Milton Nielsen, the referee. He produced the yellow card for Simeone and the red for Beckham. After Maradona in 1986, another Diego had played a crucial part in England's downfall. This time, though, they suffered at their own hands and not at those of a man who thought he was a God.

Keane ordered home after bust-up

Ireland in turmoil before World Cup

23 May 2002 | Saipan

FROM RICK BROADBENT AND GEORGE CAULKIN

When Roy Keane announced his intention to retire from international football immediately after the World Cup finals, he did it in a fashion that imitated his playing style: studs up. Furious at Ireland's build-up to the tournament, the captain decided that "enough is enough", but he cannot have expected that Mick McCarthy, the manager, would think the same. Keane was sent home from Saipan yesterday, leaving the squad a man short and a nation shorn of a hero.

The timing of his argument with McCarthy's coaching staff, his threat to quit, his subsequent about-turn and his trenchant criticism of the Football Association of Ireland (FAI) – and, by implication,

McCarthy – amounted to a challenge, one that was typically late. "I can't go on banging my head against a brick wall," he said. Now he will not have to. Instead, with replacements only allowed through serious injury, Ireland will begin their World Cup campaign in eight days with reduced numbers and diminished hopes of making the second stage.

It is extraordinary that McCarthy should consider taking the field without his one player of genuine global pedigree, but he has been pushed to the brink by Keane's behaviour. "I cannot and will not tolerate being spoken to with that level of abuse being thrown at me," he said after yesterday's clear-the-air meeting descended into "a slanging match".

Roy Keane and Ireland manager Mick McCarthy during an Ireland training session in Saipan in the build-up to the 2002 World Cup. Keane's frustration with Ireland's approach would soon boil over.

Seaman blunders when chips are down

Brazil 2 England 1

21 June 2002 | Shizouka
Quarter-final

FROM SIMON BARNES, CHIEF SPORTS WRITER

I went off David Seaman in a big way when I learnt that he signed his autographs "Safe Hands". My dear chap, surely that's for others to say. Yesterday, Safe Hands dropped the brick of his life in a career not unacquainted with bricks.

You can make a case for saying that Seaman was undone not by his own incompetence but by Ronaldinho's brilliance. It was a superb free kick: the wit behind as pleasing as the execution, a power-chip that scraped under the bar. He couldn't have placed the ball more perfectly had he carried it there rather than kicked it.

It was brilliance: but a great part of the brilliance was in spotting Seaman's incorrect position. It was not that Seaman was good and Ronaldinho was great: Ronaldinho's brilliance took the form of spotting and exploiting the weakness of his opponent.

As a member of the Goalkeepers' Union, I am more inclined to defend Seaman than not. There is an argument that Seaman took up the right position for an orthodox free kick. It was a very Seaman thing to do: play the percentages, get more right than you do wrong, when in doubt, do the bleeding obvious.

Such an approach is sound, but it fails to take genius into account. If you prepare only for the ordinary then you are likely to get undone by the extraordinary. And so the perfectly flighted free kick: and there was Seaman standing in his goal like a twitcher in a swamp: aw, I say, I wonder what that thing flying over my head is? That was the bit that was unforgivable.

In one horrific moment, England goalkeeper David Seaman realises he has misjudged Ronaldinho's free kick and the ball has gone into the net.

Vuvuzelas sound an African welcome to the world

South Africa 1 Mexico 1

11 June 2010 | Johannesburg
Group A

FROM MATTHEW SYED

Yesterday Soweto threw a party. [...] Television pictures flickered on big screens at various parks and open spaces, the shebeens rocked to the sound of vuvuzelas, and the streets were abuzz with the honking of car horns and kerbside dances. It was difficult to see a face not smiling or a bottom not being shaken.

The cause of the euphoria was the opening match of the World Cup between South Africa and Mexico, but this was about more than football. It was about a collective pride in staging one of the greatest sporting events on the planet, about a growing optimism over the chances of the national side – Bafana Bafana; above all, it was about an enduring sense of patriotism and hope despite the many broken promises of the post-apartheid era.

At Thokoza Park towards the west of the city, more than 12,000 men, women and children swayed together in a miasma of yellow and green as the clock ticked down to the opening whistle. There were more fancy dress outfits and wigs than you would find among the Barmy Army, more dancing than you would see at your average nightclub and more noise than you would hear on the Kop at Liverpool, even on a European night.

The vuvuzelas were out in force, creating a din both endearing and head-splitting. As the South African team marched on to the pitch, the instruments were thrust aloft in unison, even the three- and four-year-olds instinctively joining in. [...]

Only once during the first half did the din abate, when Mexico knocked the ball into the back of the net – but the silence rapidly turned to jubilation, when the referee ruled it offside. A large woman thrust her baby into my hands so that she could grab the nearest vuvuzela to pump out a blast.

Having a blast: a South Africa fan adds to the din – vuvuzelas made the stadiums sound like giant beehives.

Manager sacked on the eve of the tournament

Turmoil in the Spain camp

13 June 2018 | Krasnodar

FROM PAUL HIRST AND PAUL JOYCE

Spain's quest to win the World Cup descended into chaos yesterday when they fired their head coach Julen Lopetegui on the eve of the tournament.

Luis Rubiales, the president of the Royal Spanish Football Federation (RFEF), accused Lopetegui of going behind his back to set up a deal to take charge of Real Madrid after the event.

Rubiales claimed that he was only told about Lopetegui's appointment five minutes before the club made the announcement public on Tuesday.

That infuriated the president, who sacked Lopetegui yesterday, two days before Spain's opening group game against Portugal. "We cannot accept how he has acted," Rubiales told a hastily convened press conference in Krasnodar yesterday. "We only found out just five minutes before [the announcement] that he was leaving for Madrid."

Fernando Hierro, who was until yesterday the RFEF's sporting director, has been appointed head coach until the end of the tournament.

Hierro must restore order quickly if his country are to live up to their billing as one of the favourites to win the tournament. A number of senior players, including Sergio Ramos, the Spain captain, had pleaded with Rubiales to stick with Lopetegui, who was unbeaten in 20 matches in charge. "I'm very sad but I hope that we win the World Cup," Lopetegui said.

Julen Lopetegui at a Spain training session in the build-up to their World Cup opener against Portugal. The next day he was sacked.

WHAT A LINE-UP

Hungary 1954

Hungary 4 Uruguay 2

30 June 1954 | Lausanne
Semi-final

FROM GEOFFREY GREEN,
ASSOCIATION FOOTBALL CORRESPONDENT

After what must have been one of the really great matches of history, both technically and in the ration of its excitement, Hungary beat Uruguay, the holders, in the Olympic Stadium here by four goals to two. But it took the Hungarians extra time finally to impose their authority on a Uruguayan team that pushed them nearer to defeat than any side in the last four years, and who met their first defeat ever in the World Cup.

The beauty and combination of the Hungarian ground passing, as against the more forceful individual brilliance of the Uruguayans, for a long time seemed to have settled things. At the end of the opening quarter of an hour Czibor smacked home Kocsis's reverse header, a precious lead that was increased two minutes after half-time when Hidegkuti dived forward to head in a cross by Budai after swift and dexterous interplay down the right between Buzansky, Bozsik, and Kocsis.

Two up, and with only 15 minutes left, the Hungarians seemed to be home. But after the ball had twice been kicked off their goal line by Lorant, two perfect through passes bv Schiaffino suddenly saw Hohberg score twice in the last three minutes from the end of normal time, to put Uruguay level amidst fantastic scenes of enthusiasm.

In the first period of extra-time Hobherg hit the Hungarian upright a blinding smack, and from the rebound Schiaffino, almost ramming the ball home, was injured and henceforth no longer the subtle force he had been. But the Hungarians, though shaken, showed their mettle by sticking to their smooth rhythm. To win a match like this needed real football quality above all else, and character. They proved that they had both when in the last period with a replay on another day only nine minutes away, Kocsis nodded home two great goals to consummate pinpoint movements down the right.

Zoltán Czibor steers the ball past Uruguay goalkeeper
Roque Máspoli to give Hungary the lead in a classic semi-final.

Brazil 1958

Brazil 5 Sweden 2
29 June 1958 | Stockholm
Final

FROM GEOFFREY GREEN,
ASSOCIATION FOOTBALL CORRESPONDENT

Didi, floating about mysteriously in midfield, was always the master link, the dynamo setting his attack into swift motion; and, besides Didi, with Vavá and Pelé a piercing double central thrust, they had the one man above all others to turn pumpkins into coaches and mice into men – Garrincha at outside-right. Rightly has he been called the Matthews of the New World. His methods are the same: the suggestion of the inward pass, the body-swerve, the flick past the defender's left side, and the glide to freedom at an unbelievable acceleration. Poor Axbom stuck to him the best he could, but time after time he was left as lonely as a mountain wind. Garrincha, in fact, and the subtle use made of him by Didi in a swiftly changing thread of infiltration, was beyond control and that was that. There lay the most sensitive nerve-centre of the whole battle and so Brazil stretched out and grasped their ambition.

The 1958 Brazilians were not just brilliant footballers, they were good at PR, too. After their 5-2 victory over the hosts in the final, they took a Swedish flag on their lap of honour.

Brazil 1970

Brazil 4 Italy 1

21 June 1970 | Mexico City
Final

FROM GEOFFREY GREEN,
FOOTBALL CORRESPONDENT

Brazil have proved themselves the champions of champions. Theirs is a fantastic record – beaten finalists in 1950, champions in 1958 and 1962, and now champions once more. No one can hold a candle to that record; and they now kindle a hatred of only the mediocre for all such miracles.

For half the match the Italians held their own, being presented with a simple goal on a platter to keep them level at 1-1 at the interval. But they could not continue to live with this brand of Brazilian magic. There is no room for pity in football; yet at the finish one could not but feel sorry for these Italians as they drew their last breath and were burned down to the wicks of themselves. The meaning of this match fluttered above their heads, but from half-time onwards it was always out of reach as they struggled to separate the real from the unreal.

Mazzola, Riva, de Sisti and Bertini tried to shore up their crumbling fortress over the last three-quarters of an hour. But there was no escape. The Brazilians, caught in the fever of themselves, danced their way to victory as those last goals by Gérson, Jairzinho and Carlos Alberto crowned the opening strike by the world famous Pelé, now in his fourth World Cup. [...]

In spite of a casual uncertainty in defence, they have kindled as a team a spirit of oneness, especially in the flowering attack of Gérson, Rivellino, Clodoaldo in midfield, and the pressure power finishing of Pelé, Jairzinho and Tostão. They have achieved a perfect identity.

In six matches, at the end of today, they had won them all and scored 19 goals against the best of the rest of the world. That alone tells its story. Nobody has been able to live with them.

They have won because their football is a dance full of irrational surprises and Dionysiac variations. There has been no fog of fear about their game, with everybody watching for everybody else's blunders. Blunders there have been, certainly, but they made them good.

Everyone who saw them will recognise the skill factor of these Brazilians that was devastating. They were not corrupted by over usage. Best of all, perhaps, was the unshadowed enjoyment they showed in their own pleasures and their own success.

They have shown the green light to the whole field of football over the past 20 years.

Jairzinho turns away triumphantly after putting Brazil 3-1 up in their victory over Italy in the final. He is still the only player to score in every round of the competition.

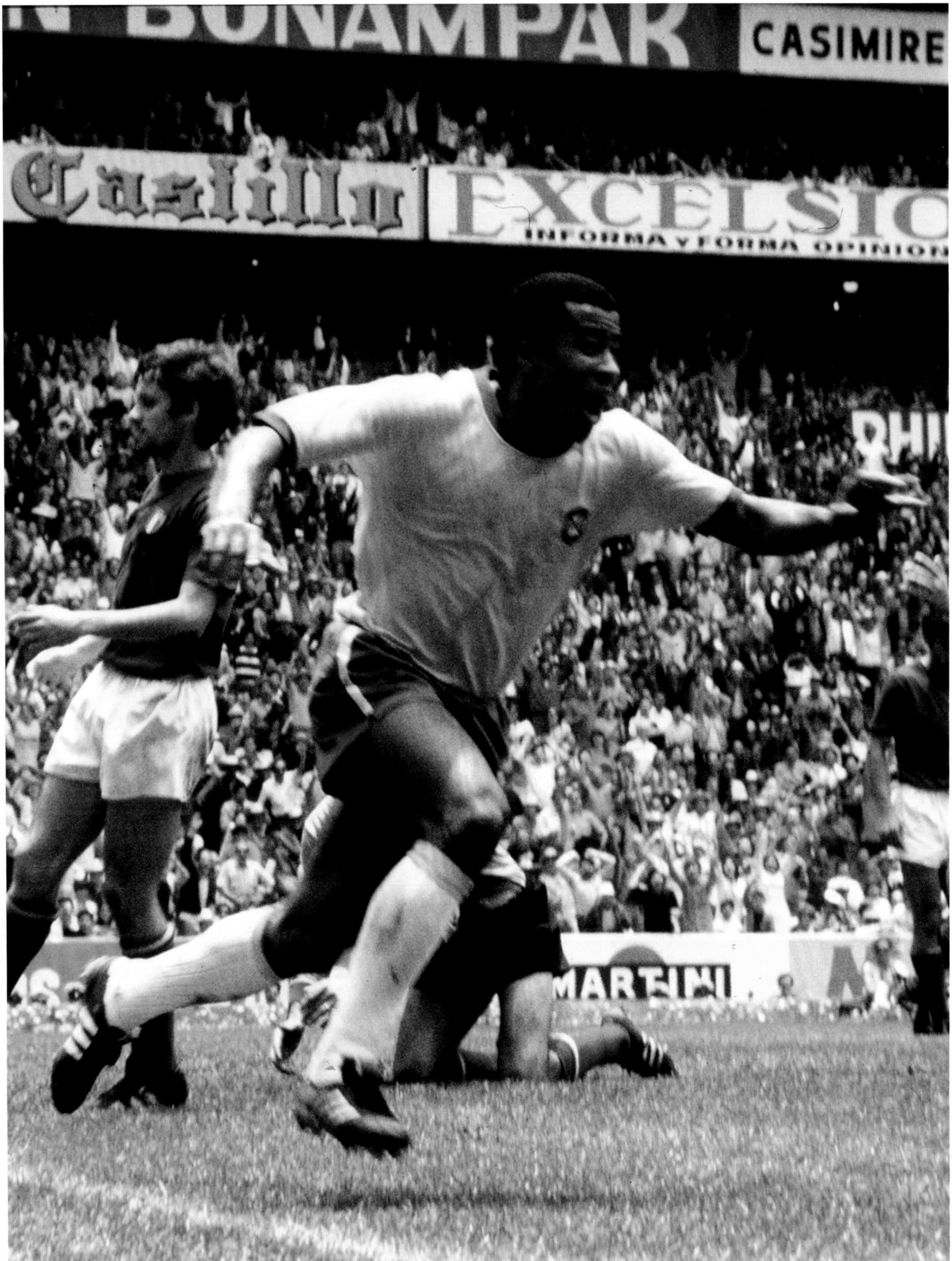
BONAMPAR
CASIMIRE
EXCELSIO
MARTINI

Netherlands 1974

Netherlands 4 Bulgaria 1

23 June 1974 | Dortmund
Group 3

FROM GERALD SINSTADT

The potential of this Netherlands side is as plain as the poise of a mannequin. Every pass, every dovetailed switch of positions has a polished elegance that few teams in the world can match. [...]

Discipline apart, the Netherlands' only weakness was the prodigality with which their finishing betrayed some wonderfully imaginative preparation. The team has been built round two of Europe's most successful club sides, Ajax and Feyenoord, and the benefit is plain in the telepathic instinct for changing positions.

Rijsbergen, playing in only his fourth international, was a coolly composed central defender. Yet when Israel arrived as a half-time substitute, Rijsbergen moved into midfield with equal facility. Surrbier, normally a full-back, judged his forays into the penalty area with the canniness of a Lawler. And Cruyff, of course, was Cruyff – multi-talented and ubiquitous.

Bulgarian defenders face unequal odds during their 4-1 defeat by the Netherlands in the final game in Group 3.

Brazil 1982

Brazil 4 Scotland 1
18 June 1982 | Seville | Group 6

FROM NORMAN FOX

With three goals in the second half, Brazil ended with the flourish every uncommitted observer of the World Cup had hoped to see. Scotland were merely praiseworthy victims. [...]

Suitably sparked into more positive action Brazil set up a series of typically flowing attacks which generally floundered on the retreating Scottish defence and midfield players. They were frustrated until the 34th minute when, not surprisingly in view of the pressure, Hansen made a cumbersome challenge on Cerezo, who seemed to run into him. Zico surveyed the wall of defenders, saw a space and a sight of net, judged the angle and curled the ball round and over the shoulders of the Scots with such uncanny skill that poor Rough was made to look foolish. [...]

Twenty minutes into the second half Brazil displayed all of their incomparable imagination. A quick breakaway saw Socrates push the ball forward to Serginho, who confused the defence by his clever, slick, forward pass. Eder was left unmarked and lifted a superb chipped shot over Rough.

*Zico, third from left, celebrates his brilliant
free-kick equaliser against Scotland.*

France 1998

France 3 Brazil 0

12 July 1998 | Paris | Final

FROM OLIVER HOLT, FOOTBALL CORRESPONDENT

They had never really been given a chance. They were to have been the fall guys, the little men against the giants of Brazil. So when the theme from *Star Wars* began to play as they waited to lift their gleaming gold trophy, the men of France, the underdogs whose bite was worse than their bark, clambered on the table in front of the assembled dignitaries to show the world that The Force had been with them all along.

Allez les Bleus: France get a nationwide party started after their unexpectedly comfortable victory over Brazil in the final.

Spain 2010

Spain 1 Germany 0

7 July 2010 | Durban
Semi-final

FROM MATT DICKINSON,
CHIEF SPORTS CORRESPONDENT

No amount of World Cup drama, or colour, can make up for the absence of a truly great team, but this tournament found its missing piece last night. Spain arrived, a little later than expected, but with a style and panache that the whole planet could cheer.

Spain have never even reached a World Cup final but, as we were once more bewitched by Xavi Hernandez and Andres Iniesta, the sense that their time has finally come was inescapable.

Either way, a new name will be engraved on the World Cup trophy on Sunday evening. We talk of England as overdue the greatest prize in sport, but that feels like an insult to Spain and Holland given their wait, and their pedigree.

We will hope for a thrilling contest but if ever a side laid claim to the trophy before the final, it is Spain. Holland, a poor man's Germany, will need to play the game of their lives and the world will turn their eyes on Johannesburg hoping that Spain's 1-0 victory last night preceded an even more spectacular performance for the crowning glory.

It has taken a while but Vicente Del Bosque's men have stirred.

After decades of underachievement, Spain finally discovered a team to take on the world in the first decade of the 21st century. They won the European Championship in 2008 and 2012 and the World Cup in between.

Germany 2014

Germany 1 Argentina 0

13 July 2014 | Rio De Janeiro
Final

FROM OLIVER KAY, CHIEF FOOTBALL CORRESPONDENT

It was just like 1990 all over again at a joyous, tear-stained Maracanã last night. A late, late goal saw Germany crowned as World Cup winners, leaving the greatest player of his generation heartbroken. The role of Diego Maradona was played, of course, by Lionel Messi. The role of Andreas Brehme was played by a gleeful Mario Götze.

Götze's goal as a substitute, seven minutes from the end of extra time, secured Germany's fourth World Cup and their first since reunification in 1990. Just like 24 years ago in Rome, they were worthy winners as the outstanding team of the tournament, even if on this occasion defeat felt harsh on an Argentina side who had at least been their equal for 90 minutes and more.

Philipp Lahm, Toni Kroos, Thomas Müller and a blood-spattered Bastian Schweinsteiger might even have been second-best over the course of the evening, but they have shown themselves over the past four weeks – and, more than that, over the past four years – to be a team of the highest class.

After the Spanish version, this is a German golden generation, worthy successors to West Germany's winners from 1954, 1974 and 1990.

At the end of a thrilling, uplifting tournament that has done much to restore international football's diminishing lustre, Germany had become the first European team to win a World Cup in South America.

The final whistle goes in Rio and Germany know they have created history as the first European team to win the trophy in South America.

Bobby Moore

Brazil 1 England 0

7 June 1970 | Guadalajara
Group 3

Strange to relate, but Geoffrey Green's *Times* report of the epic Brazil-England contest in Guadalajara made no mention of the magnificent performance of the holders' captain Bobby Moore. Others were not in doubt – his teammate Geoff Hurst put it a notch higher than his display against West Germany in the 1966 final. Bobby Charlton added: "Bobby was inspired against Brazil. He constantly broke up moves, always reading where the danger was coming from: he was just one step ahead in reading the ball and timing the tackle." One intervention in particular became celebrated above all others. In the second half, with Brazil leading 1-0, winger Jairzinho raced 40 yards, gathering pace as he went towards an undermanned England backline. Coolness personified, Moore waited his moment, delayed in fact until Jairzinho was inside the penalty area, before calmly dispossessing the rampaging winger with a perfectly timed extension of his right leg. "Like Superman stopping a runaway train," wrote Moore's biographer Matt Dickinson. In fact as Dickinson, the former *Times* football correspondent, pointed out, it was not a textbook challenge; Moore had made the interception with the wrong leg. "It still stands out as a masterly piece of defending," said Charlton.

RICHARD WHITEHEAD

England captain Bobby Moore and his Brazilian opposite number Carlos Alberto meet before a classic encounter in Mexico.

Pelé

Brazil 4 Italy 1

21 June 1970 | Mexico City
Final

The arguments will continue for as long as football is played, but for many Pelé is, and will remain, the greatest player in the history of the World Cup. The distinguished *Times* football correspondent Geoffrey Green certainly thought so. In his preview of the 1970 final – in many ways Pelé's apotheosis – he wrote of accompanying the great Brazil team on their flight from Guadalajara to Mexico City, the players apparently unconcerned by an electrical storm raging outside. "The great man slept like an extinct volcano," he wrote. "But I expect he will be awake on Sunday." He didn't disappoint, with a brilliant opening goal and what would now be recorded as assists for Jairzinho and Carlos Alberto. Yet the myth ignores the fact that injuries meant he played in only two matches in both the 1962 and 1966 tournaments and four of Brazil's six matches in 1958; 1970 was his only complete World Cup in other words. It does not matter. His shimmering brilliance in the heat and altitude of Mexico was beamed across the world in glorious technicolour, finally banishing any doubts about the uniqueness of his gifts. He retired from international football a year later with one regret – he had never scored a World Cup goal with an overhead kick.

RICHARD WHITEHEAD

All poise and power, Pelé takes on the massed ranks of the Italy defence in the 1970 World Cup final.

Johan Cruyff

Netherlands 0 Sweden 0

19 June 1974 | Dortmund
Group 3

Johan Cruyff played in only one World Cup, and he left it without a winner's medal. Yet his impact during the three weeks of the 1974 tournament in West Germany was such that his status as one of the competition's greatest stars is not in doubt. Throughout Holland's triumphant progress to the final against the hosts in Munich, he was the fulcrum of a team demonstrating the philosophy of Total Football to an admiring world. Perhaps it is odd that the single moment for which Cruyff is best remembered – throughout his career, not just at this tournament – came in an otherwise uneventful group-stage draw with Sweden. Finding himself tightly marshalled by Swedish defender Jan Olsson on the right-hand side of the penalty area, he shaped to cross but then, as Olsson moved across to block, dragged the ball away behind his supporting leg and sprinted clear of a bamboozled opponent. "That turn wasn't something I'd ever done in training or practised," Cruyff later wrote. "The idea came to me in a flash because at that particular moment it was the best solution for the situation I was in." Perhaps surprisingly, Olsson was happy to be remembered as the stooge in that moment of genius. "Johan Cruyff gave me the proudest moment of my career," he said on Cruyff's death in 2016.

RICHARD WHITEHEAD

Throughout their World Cup campaign in 1974, Cruyff was the leader and principal creative force in a superb Dutch team.

Diego Maradona

Argentina 1 Uruguay 0

16 June 1986 | Puebla
Second round

FROM DAVID MILLER

For all the criticism that has been heaped on Maradona, his talent is of a dimension which has been equalled by fewer than a dozen players in history. He is, as he was against Uruguay on Monday afternoon, truly exceptional.

There is no player in the England team, nor probably for that matter in any team, capable of subduing him head to head. He overwhelmed Barios, the Uruguayan captain, who is himself no average defensive midfield player. Maradona has not the range of gifts, in the tactical sense, possessed by former great forwards such as Di Stefano, Pelé and Cruyff, but with the ball at his feet there is more certainty that he will go past a single defender, perhaps two and sometimes three, than at any time since Pelé dominated the 1970 Mexico World Cup.

FROM STUART JONES, FOOTBALL CORRESPONDENT

With the extraordinary talent that is packed into his powerful frame, he, more than anyone else in the tournament, has the ability to change the destiny of a match. Argentina's captain has explosive speed, delicate balance, fine control and a broad imagination. He is the complete player with only one apparent flaw.

Those who watch the tie on television will notice that his right foot is employed only for the purpose of mobility. He will rarely bother to touch the ball with it. Yet his left foot is a formidable weapon that can be a steam hammer, a chisel or a scalpel as it inflicts damage.

Diego Maradona shoots for goal during Argentina's 1-0 win over Uruguay in the last 16 of his triumphant 1986 World Cup.

Paul Gascoigne

England 1 Egypt 0

21 June 1990 | Cagliari
Group F

FROM STUART JONES, FOOTBALL CORRESPONDENT

Barnes, once more showing a singular lack of urgency on the left, looked as though he required permission to take on an opponent.

Gascoigne is naturally devoid of such inhibition, as he confirmed during his inspired performance against the Netherlands, and he at least painted flashes of colour across a largely drab canvas.

FROM DAVID MILLER

Gascoigne, whose free kick brought Wright's critical goal, has been England's revelation so far, growing in stature every match at the heart of midfield. His reverse spin past Dutch defenders on the byline nearly brought victory a week ago and in two weeks he has risen from dilettante to playmaker, with a visible resolution that can partially compensate for the absence of his injured captain.

All the qualities that made Paul Gascoigne such a devastating talent are shown as he beats Egypt's Hany Ramzy.

Roger Milla

Cameroon 2 Colombia 1

23 June 1990 | Naples
Second round

FROM SIMON BARNES

World Cups always throw up intriguing people, players who catch the world's imagination for a brief moment as the tournament warms up. Normally, these fascinating exoticisms do not travel beyond the first phase of the tournament.

Normally, too, they never actually meet, never oppose each other on the field of play. But as this World Cup gathers pace, we had the supremely unlikely pairing of Cameroon and Colombia. And it was a draw that set the two scene-stealers of the World Cup on a collision course. It was to be a cataclysmic meeting.

We had Roger (pronounced in the French fashion, Cameroon being francophone) Milla, a striker who is a couple of birthdays from his 40th birthday, and René Higuita, the penalty-taking goalkeeper whose ambition is to dribble the length of the pitch and score.

The pair not only opposed each other, their meeting on the pitch decided the match.

It was a moment richly typical of all sport: low comedy was mixed with coarse-grained, but genuine, tragedy. Milla tasted the joys of being a master of the universe, while Higuita's hubris cast him to the depths of humiliation and guilt.

Milla, twice retired, is now in his footballing dotage, and acting as the Cameroonian super-sub. He has scored four times and is one behind the leading scorer in the tournament, Tomas Skuhravy of Czechoslovakia. How delicious it would be were he to finish top overall. [...]

His call-up was a hunch from no less a person than the Cameroon president, Paul Biya, who made a special request to the side's hatchet-faced Siberian manager, Valery Nepomnyaschy (I wonder what would happen if Mrs Thatcher made a similar request to Bobby Robson). Mr Biya knows his footy: Milla has had a galvanising effect on the team. [...]

Higuita yearned to galvanise his own side, and strayed further than ever from his area in his efforts to do so. The dribbling goalie advanced towards midfield, passed to Perea, who passed back and had Higuita caught in possession. The goalkeeper was brusquely tackled by Milla, who scampered off to score the second, decisive goal.

Milla's hip-swaying dances near the corner flag became his trademark goal celebration.

Ronaldo

Brazil 2 Germany 0

30 June 2002 | Yokohama
Final

FROM MATT DICKINSON,
CHIEF SPORTS CORRESPONDENT

The resurrection of Brazil and, above all, Ronaldo was celebrated with religious fervour in Yokohama yesterday as two goals from the striker brought the 17th World Cup to a conclusion that even Germany, the losers, had to accept would be cheered around the globe.

There is not a football fan who does not have a place in his heart for either the golden shirts of the game's most successful nation or the forward with the goofy smile and the ability to inflict devastation on the best defences. Ronaldo's goals yesterday capped an extraordinary personal triumph as he won the golden boot with the highest tally at a World Cup finals since Gerd Müller scored ten for West Germany in 1970. So uplifting is the tale of his recovery that it threatened to overshadow a record fifth World Cup triumph for Brazil.

Four years ago, Ronaldo walked away from the final at France 98 as a broken victim of celebrity and commercial pressure, but he finished yesterday sobbing tears of joy. Eight goals in seven games, including yesterday's brace, is not a bad record for a man who is operating at only 80 per cent of his capacity.

The timing of his return to fitness has been uncanny because, for most of the past four years, Ronaldo has been barely able to play three matches in a row. Goals in the 67th and 79th minutes, the first after capitalising on a terrible mistake by Oliver Kahn, the Germany goalkeeper, and the second a wonderful finish to a sublime move, also concluded an astonishing comeback for a squad that had come nearer than any in Brazil's history to missing the finals.

Ronaldo's two goals gave Brazil their fifth World Cup and completed a personal tale of redemption after his breakdown before the previous final four years earlier.

Zinedine Zidane

France 3 Brazil 0

12 July 1998 | Paris
Final

FROM OLIVER HOLT, FOOTBALL CORRESPONDENT

For France, though, this was a glorious night of enlightenment, the most glorious in the footballing history of their country. It was a night when the name of Zinedine Zidane took its place above even such greats as Raymond Kopa and Michel Platini.

Zidane it was who finally delivered when the world was looking to Ronaldo. The France playmaker scored with two first-half headers that effectively put the game beyond the reach of Brazil and proved to his country that his talent could blossom even on the biggest of nights.

France 3 Spain 1

27 June 2006 | Hanover
Second round

FROM OLIVER KAY

Fitting, really, that it should come to this: Zinedine Zidane, the most eminent footballer of his time, battling to keep alight the last embers of his career against Spain, the nation where his flame appeared to have burned out. Sacrilege, perhaps, but, as he took the field last night for what threatened to be the final time, it was tempting to mourn a heaven-sent talent that had been sacrificed at the altar of greed that is the modern Real Madrid.

As he summoned the last drops of energy from his ageing limbs, as he rolled back the years to slalom through the Spain defence to administer that most poignant *coup de grâce* in stoppage time, some might have seen Zidane biting the hand that had fed him. But what did Spain – or, more specifically, Real – do for Zidane, a player who thought he was arriving in the playground of the gods in Madrid, only to find, like Luís Figo, Ronaldo and David Beckham, that it declined into an absurd fantasy world where immortality must have felt like an illusion?

Fantastique: Zinedine Zidane shows off his fabulous ball control in France's 1998 quarter-final victory over Italy.

Bobby Charlton

England 2 Mexico 0

16 July 1966
Wembley Stadium, London
Group 1

GEOFFREY GREEN, FOOTBALL CORRESPONDENT

With 38 minutes gone and an endless stream of English frontal attacks flattened by Mexico's deep defensive barrier, at last there came the one moment to lift the pall of night. Peters – a success as an imaginative creator in midfield in his first World Cup match – intercepted a Mexican move in his own half. His fluent pass found Hunt, who immediately transferred to R. Charlton. Inspired instinct at that moment gripped the England man. His thinning hair streaming in the wind, he dribbled free down the middle, jinking left, then right, before suddenly unleashing a right foot thunderbolt from some 25 yards. Here was a goal to remember, Wembley thundered its applause: the Mexicans themselves remained thunderstruck.

"We want goals," the Wembley crowd had been chanting after nearly 40 goalless minutes against Mexico had followed England's 0-0 draw in the opening game against Uruguay. Then Bobby Charlton took a hand with this screamer to open the scoring against Mexico.

Pelé

Brazil 4 Italy 1

21 June 1970 | Mexico City
Final

There had been 18 minutes of sparring, each side feeling the other out, in the 1970 World Cup final before Brazil landed the first telling blow. A headed clearance went out of play near the corner flag on the left-hand touchline. Tostão's deceptively clever throw-in offered Rivellino the chance to hook a cross to back post to where Pelé was waiting. "There was Pelé, the great man erupting like a volcano, snapping his bull neck like the crack of a whip to head home violently," wrote Geoffrey Green in his *Times* match report. "That was Brazil's 100th goal in the World Cup," BBC commentator Kenneth Wolstenholme told viewers, showing off his pre-match research. It was a goal that showcased one of the lesser known weapons in Pelé's armoury – his prodigious ability in the air. "I timed my jump to perfection," he reflected later. It set the scene for a team performance of luminous brilliance under the Mexican sun.

RICHARD WHITEHEAD

Pelé celebrates the brilliant header that gave
Brazil an early lead in the 1970 final against Italy.

Carlos Alberto

Brazil 4 Italy 1

21 June 1970 | Mexico City
Final

Brazil's final flourish in their 1970 World Cup campaign was a masterclass; a stunning team goal climaxed by a thrilling individual finish. That it came from the captain who was about to receive the Jules Rimet trophy made it just that little bit more special. It began with some extravagant showboating by Clodoaldo at the back, moved to Rivellino, whose pass up the touchline to Jairzinho was the moment when the move acquired a hint of menace to the weary Italians. The winger switched the ball across to Pelé on the right-hand side of the penalty area. He did not appear even to look before stroking a nonchalant pass to Carlos Alberto coming up like an express train on his right. Such was the perfection of Pelé's apparently casual pass that the full-back did not have to break stride before smashing a fulminating shot into the opposite corner of the goal. "Carlos Alberto and I knew each other brilliantly well, on and off the pitch," Pelé explained. "We had a synchronicity and that was most delightfully demonstrated in that final World Cup goal." Carlos Alberto was equally enthusiastic. "I think it was the best goal ever scored in a World Cup," he said.

RICHARD WHITEHEAD

With the net still rippling from the impact of his shot, Carlos Alberto celebrates the stunning goal that sealed Brazil's 1970 triumph.

Diego Maradona

Argentina 2 England 1

22 June 1986 | Mexico City
Quarter-final

FROM STUART JONES, FOOTBALL CORRESPONDENT

As had been feared, Maradona, a dwarf by comparison to those around him, towered above the tie. England's defence and the whole stadium itself trembled in expectation whenever he was on the run, either twisting and weaving with the ball attached securely to his remarkable left foot or merely gliding smoothly into position.

Within a few seconds that were tucked inside the 55th minute, he scored a second goal of such dazzling beauty that it will be remembered forever by all those privileged enough to witness it. England in the end can have no complaints about effectively being knocked out by a moment of pure and irresistible genius.

Maradona, accelerating as swiftly as a bird on the wing, swayed and swerved his way past Sansom, Butcher, Fenwick and finally Shilton with effortless ease. With a nonchalant prod, he claimed not only the individual goal of the competition so far but he also ended England's journey towards the last four.

FROM DAVID MILLER

An often square back four awaited Maradona's sorties like an Indian rural village not knowing when the tiger may strike next. Butcher, who is an acceptable defender in the context of the Football League, is out of his depth at the level of a World Cup quarter-final, an honest digger of potatoes.

After the dazzling run from the halfway line, Diego Maradona sidesteps England goalkeeper Peter Shilton and delivers the coup de grâce.

David Platt

England 1 Belgium 0

26 June 1990 | Bologna
Second round

FROM STUART JONES, FOOTBALL CORRESPONDENT

David Platt, with his first goal for his country, last night lifted England clear of the most dreaded fate and into the last eight of the World Cup. Only 60 seconds were left when the second-round tie, which seemed destined to be decided cruelly by penalties, was settled by Aston Villa's prolific scorer.

Spinning as Gascoigne's free-kick dropped over his right shoulder, the substitute swung his boot and earned England the right to meet Cameroon in Naples on Sunday. The finale was spectacular and almost unbearably dramatic. Perhaps too much so. England, though elated and relieved, were also mentally drained and physically exhausted. Bobby Robson, the England manager, has five days in which to prepare his team for the 93rd international of his managerial career.

GRAHAM TAYLOR

David is not outstanding at any one thing. He has pace, but is not the quickest. He competes well in the air, but is not the highest jumper. He passes both long and short with both feet, but only occasionally delivers a pass of great perception. He does not tackle a lot because he does not have to; he positions himself to intercept instead.

He often scores with simple tap-ins but adds to his total with the occasional outstanding goal. He is a midfield player working from penalty box to penalty box, always on the move, as prepared to do "unseen" work for his colleagues as to seek glory himself. He never misses training, likes a laugh and a flutter on the horses, but he is no fool and will cope with the outside pressures and influences that international success is bound to bring.

In fact, he is the best £200,000 that I ever spent.

David Platt can hardly believe it after his volley deep in extra time takes England into the quarter-finals.

Platt poses for photographers after scoring the goal that catapulted him to international stardom.

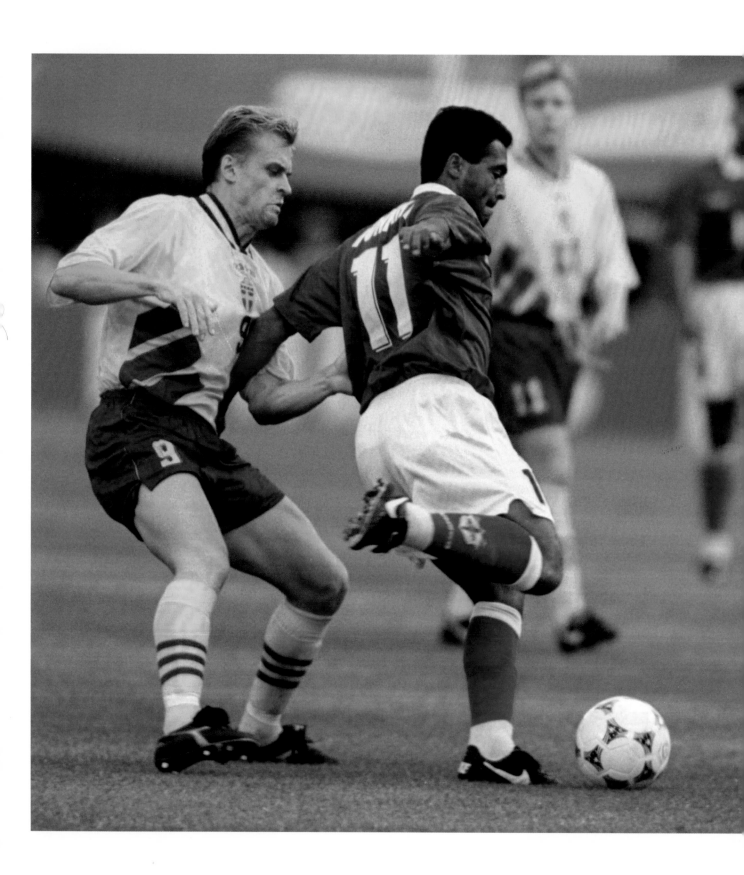

Romario

Brazil 1 Sweden 1

28 June 1994 | Detroit
Group B

FROM ROB HUGHES, FOOTBALL CORRESPONDENT

B ut the genius that Romario injects into every game took precisely one minute 38 seconds of the second half to arrive.

Americans, and there were 77,217 here in the stadium, like to talk of the assist. This time there was none. Romario gathered the ball outside the penalty area. He stopped for an instant, then propelled himself forward with that astonishing pace and low-slung balance. Three men tried to stop him, Larsson, Patrik Andersson and Arsenal's new recruit, Schwarz.

None dared to attempt a tackle, none got close enough. Romario snaked through them, and the face of Ravelli was already forlorn. The lonely goalkeeper had no ghost of a chance as the right foot propelled the ball past him low into the net. Romario is unique.

The elusive Romario proves a handful for Sweden captain Jonas Thern in the Brazil-Sweden group match in the Pontiac Silverdome.

David Beckham

England 2 Colombia 0
26 June 1998 | Lens | Group G

FROM OLIVER HOLT, FOOTBALL CORRESPONDENT

David Beckham last night answered the prayers of all those who had lamented his omission from England's two opening World Cup games when he produced a stunning performance and his first international goal here in the Stade Felix Bollaert to carry his team into the second round of the tournament.

Goals from Darren Anderton and Beckham, two men who had until last night been joined only in rivalry for one place in the side, banished the spectre of England being eliminated from the first phase of the World Cup for the first time since 1958. [...]

England went close again in the 25th minute, when another cross from Anderton was only half cleared and fell to Owen at the back post. He controlled the ball on his chest and volleyed it towards goal, but it rose just too high and cleared the Colombia crossbar.

Five minutes after that, though, England extended their lead. Ince surged forward from midfield and was brought down by Preciado 30 yards from goal. Beckham stood over the free kick with Anderton, but it was the Manchester United midfield player who ran up and curled an unstoppable right-foot shot over the wall, the ball arrowing just inside Mondragon's right-hand post.

It was his first goal for England in 15 appearances and he celebrated with the gusto it deserved, running towards the England fans high in the stands behind the goal and savouring their cheers of rapture.

David Beckham hits a perfect free kick over the Colombia wall to give England a 2-0 lead in their must-win final group game.

Michael Owen

England 2 Argentina 2
(Argentina won 4-3 on penalties)
30 June 1998 | St Étienne
Second round

FROM KEVIN McCARRA

Within moments of the kick-off, their defenders could vouch for Owen's uncanny maturity, since, in the third minute, it had forced Roberto Ayala to go sliding in on the seat of his pants to make a blocking tackle. Although England were still to fall behind, that moment was the kernel from which the must of the first-half action grew.

The Napoli player is a sweeper, detailed to linger behind two centre backs and act as a fail-safe mechanism should an opponent break clear. Owen, however, often made it appear that Ayala was the first, and only, line of defence. His pace burnt off José Chamot and Nelson Vivas before either man could close in on him. The acceleration makes him dangerous in a variety of ways.

In the attack that brought England's penalty kick, Ayala was fearful of making the contact that can easily knock over a hurtling figure, but in his hesitation he could not quite avoid the faint brush that sent Owen to the ground. Too much, all the same, can be made of his sprinting. If only that quality were required, scouts would haunt athletics fields rather than youth football matches.

It is Owen's ability to direct his pace that is really precious. His goal was composed of high-speed poise as he raced away from Chamot, took a course round Ayala that still left him with a favourable angle to shoot and then clipped the ball carefully clear of Carlos Roa, the goalkeeper. It is conventional, and even reasonable, to gasp with anticipation at the thought of a fully-developed Owen.

Catch me if you can: Michael Owen prepares to round defender Roberto Ayala on his way to scoring a brilliant individual goal.

Dennis Bergkamp

Netherlands 2 Argentina 1

4 July 1998 | Marseille
Quarter-final

FROM OLIVER HOLT, FOOTBALL CORRESPONDENT

If there can be any divinity in the concept of retribution, then it appeared three minutes from the end of a World Cup quarter-final in the Stade Velodrome here early on Saturday evening. With his blond hair and his blue eyes, Dennis Bergkamp unleashed himself on Argentina like an avenging angel and brought England some vicarious pleasure in Dutch joy. [...]

Ortega's own moment of madness, after he appeared to have been tripped in the box by Stam, helped Holland on their way but it took Bergkamp to push them into the semi-finals with a goal that ranked with the collector's items he scored in Arsenal's charge towards the double last season. He had already thrilled the orange hordes in the stadium with a sublime piece of skill that set up the first Holland goal in the twelfth minute. [...]

Then, after the dismissals, and as the match moved into injury time, Frank de Boer sent a 50-yard pass over the defence to Bergkamp. The Arsenal striker controlled it effortlessly with his first touch and pushed it inside Ayala with his second. Then he swung the outside of his right boot at the ball and sent it curling beyond Roa high into the net.

Dennis Bergkamp cuts back inside Argentina defender Roberto Ayala before delivering a brilliant finish to give the Netherlands a last-minute quarter-final victory.

Esteban Cambiasso

Argentina 6
Serbia & Montenegro 0

16 June 2006 | Gelsenkirchen
Group C

FROM OLIVER KAY

So captivating is the sight of Diego Maradona, proudly waving his nation's colours among the suits in the corporate seats, that Argentina's players might occasionally have felt like a sideshow act at this World Cup, rather than the main attraction. Not yesterday, though, as a performance of breathtaking brilliance in Gelsenkirchen, illuminated by one of the most stunning goals in the tournament's history, confirmed them as serious contenders to follow in the footsteps of the great man.

This, after the drudgery served up by England in Nuremberg the previous evening, was football at its most beautiful, a mesmerising exhibition of one-touch play to which Serbia and Montenegro's defence, supposedly one of the strongest in Europe, had no answer. The apex came on the half-hour, as a flowing 24-pass move was finished off in fitting style by Esteban Cambiasso. It is no exaggeration to say that the goal, in its conception, rivalled that scored by Brazil's Carlos Alberto in the 1970 final, recently voted the best in the 76-year history of the World Cup. Maradona might argue that his solo effort against England in Mexico City 20 years ago was the finest of all, but he cannot disguise his enthusiasm for his successors.

With a sweetly struck finish, Esteban Cambiasso rounds off a dazzling 24-pass move in Argentina's rout of Serbia & Montenegro.

Robin van Persie

Netherlands 5 Spain 1

13 June 2014 | Salvador
Group B

By the end of the rerun of the bitterly contested 2010 World Cup final, it was hard to recall that Holland had been trailing when Robin van Persie scored this beautiful goal. When the final whistle blew, the holders had been comprehensively thrashed by a dazzling display of Dutch football. "Four years, it seems, is a very long time indeed," wrote Rory Smith in his *Times* match report. "It is certainly a long time to wait for revenge. Holland have that now, in a fashion that stretches beyond their wildest dreams." Xabi Alonso had given Spain the lead from the penalty spot after 27 minutes, but Holland set the scene for their second-half rampage by drawing level a minute before half-time. Daley Blind spotted Van Persie's perfectly timed run and struck a fabulous lofted pass into the penalty area. But it was what happened next that elevated the goal to greatness. The Manchester United striker, evading Spain's offside trap, spotted Iker Casillas was off his line and, with a deceptively simple looking flick of his head, lofted a perfect header over the stranded goalkeeper from 16 yards. "There are times when football creates moments of such beauty that you struggle to catch your breath," wrote columnist Matthew Syed a few days later.

RICHARD WHITEHEAD

Robin van Persie launches himself forward to guide a perfect header over Spain goalkeeper Iker Casillas for the Netherlands' equaliser.

Tim Cahill

Australia 2 Netherlands 3

18 June 2014 | Porto Alegre
Group B

It was quite a way to go out. In what turned out to be his last World Cup match, Australia's Tim Cahill struck a goal of awesome power in his country's 3-2 defeat by the Dutch. It brought Australia level at 1-1 in the 21st minute, straight after Arjen Robben had given Holland the lead. Cahill, well known to English viewers after his spells at Millwall and Everton, demonstrated a potent mixture of skills to score a goal described as "barnstorming" by James Ducker in his match report. First, Cahill had to keep an unblinking eye on a long pass floated from midfield into the path of his run. Then he had to execute one of the most difficult skills in the game: volleying a ball with his left foot that had dropped from the sky over his right shoulder. He did it perfectly; sending a 14-yard shot rocketing into the net via the underside of the bar. A booking later in the game meant a suspension for Australia's final group game and also his substitution just after the hour. But he had plenty to remember. "I play for the moment and I have had five of the best moments of my life in the World Cup," he said.

RICHARD WHITEHEAD

Tim Cahill, far right, makes sweet contact with a crashing volley to sent the ball into the Netherlands' net via the crossbar.

James Rodríguez

Colombia 2 Uruguay 0

28 June 2014 | Rio de Janeiro
Second round

FROM RORY SMITH

There are three goals, one for each act, in the rise of James Rodríguez. He was 12 when he scored the first. It came in the Liga Pony, Colombia's most illustrious youth tournament. [...]

The second came six years later. Rodríguez was not quite 19, playing for Banfield, one of Argentina's lesser lights. He chose them ahead of the more famous Boca Juniors partly because "they believed in young players" and partly because they played in the same colours as the team he supported as a child, Atlético Nacional in Medellin. Banfield are playing Lanus. The first half is drawing to a close. Rodríguez skips down the left wing and cuts inside. He races, unchallenged, to the edge of the six-yard box, only the goalkeeper in his way. He scoops the ball, skimming it really, over a flailing arm and into the far corner. [...]

The third came on Saturday evening, for his country, against Uruguay in the Maracanã. It is the sort of goal you can watch again and again. The rapid glance to see precisely where Fernando Muslera, the Uruguay goalkeeper, is standing; the chest control, on the edge of the box; the picture-perfect left-foot volley to send the ball arcing over Muslera's outstretched right arm, off the underside of the crossbar and in. That was the goal that made him a star.

Remember the name: James Rodríguez celebrates after scoring in Colombia's last-16 victory over Uruguay.

Toni Kroos

Germany 2 Sweden 1
23 June 2018 | Sochi | Group F

FROM IAN HAWKEY

Toni Kroos looked up, briefed Marco Reus about precisely where he wanted the ball teed up and glanced beyond the Swedish wall, beyond the goalkeeper, beyond the improbable angle and apparently beyond the next three rounds of a World Cup he was about to rescue.

"If we show as much fight as this, we'll deserve to reach the final," Kroos said smiling. He had arrowed in his stunning, stoppage-time goal to deliver for Germany – who had trailed Sweden at half-time and were down to ten men – their first points of the tournament. It felt like a sign, and if the lurid celebrating by some members of the German staff on the touchline spoke of a pent-up emotion, there is an instinct among the players to harness Saturday night's epic escape as a powerful springboard.

The champions had stood on the brink, their short-term destiny in this World Cup beyond their control as the clock ticked past 94 minutes in Sochi. Kroos's dead-ball expertise put them back on track, albeit in a direction that deviates slightly from the original masterplan.

Toni Kroos has just struck a pitch-perfect shot to send the ball arrowing into the opposite corner of the goal and give Germany a last-gasp victory over Sweden that kept their World Cup hopes alive.

Lionel Messi

Argentina 2 Nigeria 1

26 June 2018 | St Petersburg
Group D

FROM MATT DICKINSON, CHIEF SPORTS WRITER

Argentina came to scrap for their lives but all knew that their fate would depend largely on one man, just as it had in reaching Russia, reliant on a Messi hat-trick to win in Ecuador and avoid missing a first World Cup finals since 1970.

"We have the best player in the world and the rest need to benefit from that," [coach, Jorge] Sampaoli said. "That's why I said the match against Croatia was our problem, not his problem." Messi certainly started like a man on a mission.

He had just 49 touches in defeat by Croatia. He had passed that number by half-time here, including that sumptuous goal.

It was his first of the tournament with his 13th shot and made him the first player to score a World Cup goal in his teens, twenties and thirties – not even Pelé did that, being 29 in 1970 – to add to all the squillions of other record-breaking stats.

And it was delivered with such characteristic brilliance and deftness, controlling Éver Banega's beautifully flighted pass from the halfway line with one touch of the thigh, dabbing the ball forward with his left foot before rifling his shot across Francis Uzoho with his right. Wrong foot? Do not insult the maestro.

Up in the stands, Maradona crossed his arms over his chest and exclaimed something about God. For once, presumably he was not referring to himself.

Lionel Messi gives thanks after his sublime skills allowed him to score one of the goals of the tournament for Argentina against Nigeria.

Kieran Trippier

England 1 Croatia 2

11 July 2018 | Moscow
Semi-final

FROM HENRY WINTER, CHIEF FOOTBALL WRITER

The man of the first half was Trippier, arguably England's man of the tournament, who picked the perfect moment to score his first goal for his country. Lingard pirouetted away from Ivan Rakitic, cutting inside and releasing Dele Alli into the soft belly of Croatia's defence. His speed caught out Luka Modric, who brought him down 25 yards out.

Trippier had prepared for these moments ever since he was in the Manchester City youth team, getting the mannequins out after training at Platt Lane, working with the coach Steve Ayre, honing his free-kick technique. He studied David Beckham at length, practised at Spurs with Christian Eriksen and that illustrious pair would have been proud of what happened next.

Trippier's strike, sent at pace over the wall, clearing Lovren and Mandzukic, seemed almost to kiss the air and wink at Danijel Subasic as it continued its regal journey past the Croatia goalkeeper, who reacted far too late and then bizarrely shrugged at the goal.

With perfect execution, Kieran Trippier curls his free kick over the Croatia wall to give England an early lead in the semi-final.

Nat Lofthouse dives just inches from the ground to head Tom Finney's cross past Belgium goalkeeper Leopold Gernaey and put England 2-1 ahead.

Lofthouse leads the line in epic tussle

Belgium 4 England 4

17 June 1954 | Basel | Group 4

FROM GEOFFREY GREEN,
ASSOCIATION FOOTBALL CORRESPONDENT

England, throwing away victory and drawing with Belgium here tonight at four goals all after extra time in their opening match in the World Cup, were like those rare children of light who can pass through any experience protected by a sheath of impenetrable innocence.

Their experience came at the very beginning – a dark cloud of foreboding – which saw Belgium take a sudden lead at the fifth minute. Their innocence later lay in a belief that they were home and dry by 3-1 with only a quarter of an hour left. But as dusk softened the receding day a dramatic violence fell on the scene. Belgium scored twice within the closing minutes to draw level at 3-3, and at the end of a further half-hour two weary sides struck by cramp with another goal each dragged themselves from the battlefield still locked in equal combat.

So once more one must wipe away a tear for England on a foreign field. And this time it was a bitter tear, for after shaking that opening cloud off their shoulders they dominated the central hour with some pure cultured football to take a lead that should have given them a worthy victory. Yet the end turned back to hold hands with the beginning, and England sadly threw away the palm that was in their grasp. And the bitterest touch of all came during extra time when the unhappy Dickinson headed a long free kick from Dries past Merrick to put Belgium level for the last time, after Lofthouse had only two minutes earlier scored England's fourth goal from a true pass engineered by Taylor and Broadis.

Merseyside hails the modern Magyars

Hungary 3 Brazil 1

15 July 1966 | Goodison Park,
Liverpool | Group 3

FROM GEOFFREY GREEN,
ASSOCIATION FOOTBALL CORRESPONDENT

This was a night to remember for any one of the 51,000 people at Goodison Park, Everton – and certainly a night no Hungarian, however far from Merseyside, will forget. There must have been dancing in the streets of Budapest when the news came through, laughter even in the waters of the Danube. Just as there must have been a dark, disbelieving pall of gloom descending on every home and forest and mountain in far-off Brazil.

This was the first defeat of the world champions in any World Cup match for 12 years, a span which has seen them take a firm hold of the golden trophy of Jules Rimet. That was in 1954, the "battle of Berne", an infamous match the game of football and all those of us who saw it have always done our best to forget. Here, instead, was a game of shimmering beauty, set to grace any World Cup final, where both sides, it seemed, set out with one intention only. That was to wipe out the past and to reveal football in all its most beautiful and heroic colours.

From the very start it had a throb: first the throb of a tom-tom high in the stands that might have come from some jungle on the banks of the Amazon: then a throb of the heart as battle was joined and the Hungarians began to show their glorious capabilities. Very soon, too, Hungary's scintillating reply found an ally. It was found in the voice of the Merseyside crowd. "Hun-ga-ry! Hun-ga-ry!" came the roar. lt might have been "Liv-er-pool" or "Ev-er-ton". And soon also to it was added "Ee-ay-addyo!" That is the way of an English crowd, standing neutral but now firmly behind the supposed underdogs.

*Janos Farkas celebrates
after his brilliant volley
gave Hungary a 2-1 lead.*

England's heroic captain Bobby Moore is raised aloft by his exhausted teammates after England's extra time triumph.

England climb to the summit

England 4 West Germany 2

30 July 1966 | Wembley Stadium, London | Final

BY GEOFFREY GREEN,
ASSOCIATION FOOTBALL CORRESPONDENT

England, the pioneers of organised football and the home of the game, are the new World Champions for the first time. They are still pinching themselves.

So, too, are others of us, the sceptics, who from the start thought the feat beyond our reach. But it is no dream. If England, perhaps, did not possess the greatest flair, they were the best prepared in the field, with the best temperament based on a functional plan. Further to that, they built up to a peak. The timing of it was good.

West Germany, twice semi-finalists in other years and the surprise holders of 1954, when they upset the magnificent Hungarians, were beaten fair and square in a match of high drama. A squally afternoon of showers and sunshine was rich with excitement and some passing controversy that tested the stamina and willpower of both sides, to say nothing of the 93,000 crowd ranged around Wembley's steep banks and the 400 million others watching on television around the world.

The climax came in a punishing period of an extra half-hour after the Germans had first led and then saved their necks with an equalising goal at 2-2 a mere 15 seconds from the end of normal time.

To have the Cup thus apparently dashed from their lips at the very moment of victory was a deep test of England's morale. Psychologically Germany should have had the edge in that extra time. But Moore and his men rose magnificently to the challenge. Only the two sets of actors down on that green stage could have truly felt the bitter disappointment or the elation of that moment.

But as England were yet girding themselves for the extended test Mr Ramsey, their manager, walked calmly among his men to say: "All right. You let it slip. Now start again!" They did. They reacted vigorously. How some of them found the resilience and the stamina finally to outstay a German side equally powerful physically, equally determined, equally battle-hardened, was beyond praise.

All were heroes: none more so than Moore as he drove his side on; than the little flame-haired Ball, a real ball of fire this great day, as he covered every blade of grass on Wembley's wide spaces; than the intelligent Peters, than Hurst – preferred to Greaves at the eleventh hour as a striker – who crashed in two goals during extra-time to become the first man to hit the net three times in a World Cup final.

For Hurst, for Moore, the captain, and for Ramsey, the inscrutable manager, this indeed was a storybook ending. If there are no substitutes for gods, equally there are no substitutes for courage and temperament. England had those in full measure.

Thus the 1966 championships were crowned worthily in the presence of the Queen and the Duke of Edinburgh. Earlier irritations were forgotten and the best now lingers on. And never has Wembley itself provided a more emotional setting. From early afternoon the atmosphere was electric. It fairly crackled. The terracing was a sea of waving flags, the standards of two nations; the noise was a wall of sound that drowned the flutterings of one's heart. High in the stands there came the beating of a drum, a deep, pulsating thud, almost tribal.

It set the mood of a throbbing match, climaxed in the sunshine of the end when the Germans, honourable losers, made their own farewell lap of the stadium to a warm reception and followed amid thunderous roars as the stadium rose to Moore holding the golden, winged trophy in triumphal circuit. Honour and justice were done in that proud moment beyond many dreams.

So for the sixth time in eight World Cup finals the side that scored first were finally vanquished. It was the Germans who thus followed history when they broke the ice at the 13th minute. The pitch, made treacherous by two earlier showers, was ripe for error. At that moment Wilson, misjudging his leap to Seeler's deep cross from the left, headed down to the feet of Haller and there was the No.8 – one of Germany's telling factors at the side of Overath, Beckenbauer, Held, and Seeler – to steer home a quick diagonal shot beyond Banks's groping fingers.

That tiny error opened the way. Wilson quickly pushed the incident to the back of his mind and though Germany, by the interval, could claim a slight advantage in possession and use of the ball it was England that had quickly drawn level – within six minutes, in fact. An infringement by Overath on Moore brought a free kick to the left; England's captain, quickly spotting a gap in the square formation of the German defence, instantly floated a 35-yard kick through the middle and there was Hurst, again making yards from the right as he had done a week earlier against Argentina, to guide in his header.

There, at 1-1, it stood at half-time with several other narrow squeaks survived at each end. Once, Banks somehow made two point-blank, reflex saves in as many seconds from Overath and Emmerich; at the other end Tilkowski parried a left foot rocket from Hunt as Peters freed his man.

More slanting rain greeted the start of the second half, glinting through the sunshine to say that somewhere there was a fox's wedding. For a spell the struggle marked time as the opposing forces regrouped for the breakthrough. The crowd, still vibrant, sang "Oh my, what a referee!" as the Swiss made some pernickety decisions. Bobby Charlton, following a deep cross from Peters on the left, once missed the far post by a whisker. Only 18 minutes remained then. But that tribal drum began to throb again and almost at once England answered its call.

With 13 minutes to go Ball, the effervescent, the irrepressible, often tackling back to help the defence like Bobby Charlton, now forced a corner on the right. He took the kick himself: the ball, helped on, reached Hurst, whose first-time shot was blocked by Hottges. Suddenly, there was Peters all alone with the rebound in front of Tilkowski and the next second his shot billowed the net. It was West Ham United again.

That was it, we thought. Wembley shuddered like some great monster turning in its sleep. But the Germans were not done yet. Stiles, Moore and the rest covered England's rear as even the fair-haired Schnellinger came up to reinforce the last efforts of the tireless Haller, Overath, Held and Beckenbauer.

With the last minute already unwinding itself the Cup was almost in Moore's grasp. Then it happened.

Despair for England in the final moments as Wolfgang Weber slides in to equalise and send the match into extra-time.

One moment England's balloon of hope was floating gaily, or with the appearance of gaiety. The next, pop, there it was, a wrinkled sad thing upon the floor.

An infringement, wrongly, I think, given against Jack Charlton's header as Seeler made a back for him, led to Emmerich blasting his free kick into the wall of English defenders. Held blazed at the rebound, the ball spun across Banks's goalmouth – not without a suspicion of German hands on the way – and suddenly Weber was on hand to win a melee at close range as he joyfully shot Germany level.

Those bitter 15 seconds might have destroyed England, as they just had time to kick-off before the start of extra-time. But they did not. Rolling up their sleeves and turning down their stockings as the threat of cramp drew near on the porous pitch they stuck to their planned approach. Moore and Stiles, blandly shrewd, mopping up the German central thrusts; Bobby Charlton and Peters providing from midfield; Ball, unbelievably, everywhere like a wasp; Hurst and Hunt the hammer men at the front.

To add to the swaying excitement of a match of tiny errors punished there came one final point for debate. Extra time approached its mid-way as Stiles, now a five-barred gate, set Ball free with a long pass down the right. Over came the instant centre, Hurst trapped, swivelled and thundered his shot to the underside of Tilkowski's crossbar. The ball hurtled down to be headed clear by Weber.

Was it over the line or not? It was all a matter of speed of eye. It looked good.

The referee consulted his Russian linesman. The wait was agonising. The answer was "goal!" The Germans protested as England, 3-2 ahead, rejoiced and the stadium erupted.

How both sides saw out the last stages of a punishing two hours was beyond praise. But the final stroke of all was perhaps the best as the book was snapped shut. Again with only seconds to go it was England's turn to write finis to it all.

Again it was Hurst who did so imperiously. In another West Ham move he took a deep pass from Moore through the extended German defensive lines – now committed to last despairing attack – drove himself onwards to end with a rasping left foot shot that rattled Tilkowski's net.

The matter was decided, dismissed. England's players had proved Ramsey right. The Cup belonged to them and later they belonged to the jubilant, chanting crowds of the capital on what was another VE night.

Bobby Moore, in command of the situation as always, was at his imperious best in the final.

A classic encounter under the midday sun

Brazil 1 England 0

7 June 1970 | Guadalajara
Group 3

FROM GEOFFREY GREEN, FOOTBALL CORRESPONDENT

By their narrow victory with a goal from the ever dangerous Jairzinho, before the 75,000 full house at Jalisco Stadium here today, Brazil have now moved more firmly to the top of Group 3 in the World Cup.

Brazil now have both feet in the quarter-final round, where I duly expect England to join them with a concluding victory over their last opponents next Thursday, Czechoslovakia. That, however, lingers in the future.

Meanwhile, we never seem able to beat these Brazilians. In eight meetings so far, we have won only once, and that at Wembley in the 1950s. As it is, Brazil picked their fifth win against England as though in a matter of sheer chances it was something like picking a man's pocket. England, this day, in the mere matter of chances, might well have won and certainly drawn. But that is to cry over spilt milk. If you cannot take what there is to offer in this game then you must pay the price.

Over the last stages, when Moore and his men bent their every fibre to rescue their cause, Ball and Astle – what a blinding error of his as he must have closed his eyes close in before an open goal – both missed fine chances. And then, again, as time ran out, there was Ball again with bad luck, that time to hit the Brazilian crossbar.

Still, it was no abdication in a match of endless activity. The Brazilians got the bit between their teeth for a magical spell just after the interval. But England's foolproof, sound defensive game never allowed the foe to run away with it. [...]

In simple terms, here was a match between a better team, England, and better creative artists, Brazil. These Brazilians are a currency that no foreign exchange can control. When all seems at peace, and the opposition is lulled into a sense of safety, in a flash they can spread the game before their opponents like the evidence of a case. So it was on this occasion when Pelé, Jairzinho, Tostão and Rivellino suddenly produced the rabbit out of the hat.

Jairzinho runs away to celebrate the only goal of the game, leaving Martin Peters and Terry Cooper helpless.

West Germany reign supreme

West Germany 1 Poland 0

3 July 1974 | Frankfurt
Second round, Group B

FROM GEOFFREY GREEN, FOOTBALL CORRESPONDENT

West Germany, needing only to draw, went one better than that at the Wald stadium here this evening to beat Poland by a single goal from Müller a quarter of an hour from the end to reach their second final in the last three World Cups.

It was a dramatic evening played through thunder, lightning and rain which in other circumstances might well have seen the match abandoned. As it was, both sides struggled bravely through the storm, with Poland giving a final flicker as they searched for that last stride that might have taken them to Munich. Central to the issue were the conditions. The pitch was a paddy field, with mud in certain sectors where the ball had to be dug out by the players. Yet in spite of the terrible surface, both sides played the match in

a fine spirit and the Poles the losers, having had the best of the opening half, proved a credit to themselves and to the competition as a whole.

An hour before the match was to begin the storm broke. Thunder and lightning played overhead as the clouds burst. Soon the pitch was a lake and the start was delayed for half an hour while mechanical squeegees tried to clear the water.

In spite of all this, here was a match that gained an alpha-plus. Both sides were like long distance runners, with mind and breath only for the race. Some of the skills in these conditions were breathtaking, with Poland, until half-time, the more objective, progressive and down to earth side, using old-fashioned wingers with speed.

The final whistle has gone and the celebrations can begin at a soggy Frankfurt – West Germany are through to their home World Cup final.

Gemmill restores Scotland's wounded pride

Scotland 3 Netherlands 2

11 June 1978 | Mendoza | Group 4

FROM NORMAN FOX, FOOTBALL CORRESPONDENT

Scotland's disastrous World Cup ended here today with a welcome touch of defiance and a token victory that came too late to erase all of the bad memories. Beaten by Peru, held by Iran, they were finally eliminated because they were unable to score the three clear goals that they needed against the Dutch. But there were times tonight when it seemed they might achieve an astonishing recovery.

With the adventurous Souness brought into the team to give purpose to the midfield section, the Scots played football of a quality that had it come earlier would undoubtedly have taken them into the second round with the Dutch. Now, they are out on goal difference. Nevertheless, they owed an apology and in the shadows of the Andes they lightened their own black depression. This was a performance to leave the Scottish supporters saying "If only...", but at least some of them were singing again. [...]

At that moment Scotland summoned a little more of their faded pride and it carried them on with football that had it been seen earlier in the competition would surely have saved them much of their heartache. Suddenly, Gemmill was involved again – he was rarely out of the spotlight. Collecting the ball just outside the penalty area, he dodged and weaved inside and out of the apparently solid line of defenders and struck a marvellous shot past a thoroughly beaten goalkeeper. It was certainly among the finest goals of the competition, and so ironic.

Archie Gemmill, an inspiration for Scotland throughout, hurdles over a challenge from Ruud Krol.

Rossi shoots down the Brazilian maestros

Italy 3 Brazil 2

5 July 1982 | Barcelona
Second round, Group C

FROM NORMAN FOX

Still attempting to play the elegant, eloquent football of their tradition, Brazil last night departed the World Cup. Italy beat them fairly and cleverly with three goals from the irresistible Paulo Rossi.

The World Cup will be the poorer for Brazil's failure to reach a semi-final match with Poland on Thursday but Italy, if they continue to concentrate on their skills rather than their unattractive strength, can still be a credit to the tournament.

Yesterday, however, they were at a disadvantage. To reach the last four they had to win; Brazil required only a draw. The urgency of the situation brought them out of their defensive, abrasive inner character and they punished Brazil for a performance marginally less vivacious than before.

Brazil were no strangers to the situation they found themselves in after only five minutes. Against Scotland and Soviet Union they conceded early goals and recovered in style. Here they had begun by trying to avoid Italian tackles with light-stepping, one-touch football but they were soon on their heels.

Paulo Rossi, whose form had been wretched in Italy's early games, became a national hero with the hat-trick that sank the highly fancied Brazilians.

France keep their cool to extinguish Brazil's hopes

France 1 Brazil 1

(France won 4-3 on penalties)
21 June 1986 | Guadalajara
Quarter-final

FROM DAVID MILLER

It is doubtful if the first half-century of the World Cup saw a more eventful match than Saturday's quarter-final between France and Brazil. And the second half-century will be fortunate to see its equal. The two teams defied the ferocious temperature of 120 degrees in the Jalisco Stadium, and each other, to re-invigorate international football with a classic tussle which will be talked about for years. [...]

Over two hours and a half, including the wretched necessity for the nevertheless spellbinding execution by penalty shoot-out, there were the dramatic qualities of many sports. No 15-round world title bout, nor match-play golf taken to the 19th, nor five-set tennis final fluctuating on every point, nor Olympic race decided in the last few strides, nor Test won in the last over could have had more suspense.

It was one of those rare occasions which makes my occupation uniquely pleasurable, yet how to recapture the emotions, skills and courage which flowed back and forth across the sunlit pitch? I have not seen a better match in eight finals, nor one played in such a marvellous spirit: only one single mean foul, sheer desperation by Carlos, the Brazil goalkeeper late in extra-time, amid mutual generosity which put many teams here to shame. As in all great sporting moments, the quality of the losers contributed as much or more than that of the winners. How we grieve for Brazil: such a flourish, yet no reward other than admiration.

The match swung from end to end throughout, almost with the rapidity of ice hockey, and one knew not how the players sustained the momentum in their fifth match at altitude in three weeks. There were 16 scoring opportunities created by Brazil to 15 by France. In some matches there are none.

Michel Platini celebrates his equaliser – a tap-in at the far post – in a thrilling struggle between his French team and Brazil.

No way through for German marksman Miroslav Klose
as he attracts the attention of three Italian defenders.

Italy's late gatecrashers spoil the party

Italy 2 Germany 0

4 July 2006 | Dortmund
Semi-final

FROM MATT DICKINSON,
CHIEF FOOTBALL CORRESPONDENT

A shaft of light pierced the black clouds over the whole of Italian football last night as the national team advanced to the World Cup final with a stunning and deserved late victory over the tearful hosts.

Made sick on a daily diet of stories about corruption and match-fixing in the past couple of months, Italy fans instead celebrated goals deep into extra time from Fabio Grosso and Alessandro Del Piero, the latter with the last kick of the match. More than half the starting XI, including the magnificent trio of Fabio Cannavaro, Andrea Pirlo and Gennaro Gattuso, will have heard during the day that a prosecutor had demanded relegation from Serie A for their clubs in a Rome courtroom. [...]

They were the superior team and, even if it took until the 119th minute to beat Jens Lehmann, it was reward for Marcello Lippi's adventurous substitutions. He finished with four strikers, which must be a record for Italy, although it was understandable if he wanted to avoid penalties. Italian players relish shoot-outs about as much as the English and the German spot-kick machine undoubtedly would have been expected to triumph from 12 yards.

To have the game snatched from them so late was heartbreaking for Jurgen Klinsmann's team after a fine run to the last four, but while they carved out some of the game's best chances, they had overachieved in knocking out Argentina in the previous round. Their midfield, including a quiet Michael Ballack, was outmanoeuvred by Gattuso and Pirlo. Italy might have won earlier had Lippi gone for the kill before extra time.

Seven-goal Germany plunge a nation into despair

Germany 7 Brazil 1

8 July 2014 | Belo Horizonte
Semi-final

FROM OLIVER KAY, CHIEF FOOTBALL CORRESPONDENT

It was a masterclass, a thumping, a humiliation. It was an extraordinary result that did not just secure Germany's place in the World Cup final but plunged Brazilian football into darkness as their crowd went from hope, to shock, to deflation, to anger, to derision and then, briefly, to respect for their awe-inspiring conquerors.

When Andre Schurrle struck the magnificent seventh Germany goal with 11 minutes remaining, the Brazilian supporters applauded, as if to say that they, of all fans, can recognise and appreciate the class that abounds through Philipp Lahm, Toni Kroos and the rest of this team. Then the mood darkened again at the final whistle as Luiz Felipe Scolari and his similarly beleaguered players faced the wrath that inevitably followed this pathetic, shambolic capitulation.

Germany were brilliant, breaking intelligently and clinically again and again to rush into a 5-0 lead inside an astonishing first half-hour. As magnificently as Germany played, though, scoring through Thomas Müller, Miroslav Klose, Kroos, Kroos again and Sami Khedira, their task was facilitated by a complete defensive breakdown from this Brazil team who, following their hearts and losing their heads, suffered the implosion that had never seemed far away during this World Cup.

David Luiz, captain for the night, had held aloft the shirt of the unfortunate, absent Neymar beforehand. It was a nice touch, but what a joke. Luiz evidently has no more self-awareness than positional awareness, because Thiago Silva was a far bigger loss to Brazil. In the absence of their best defender and their star centre forward, Scolari's team were hopeless and Luiz confirmed his popular billing as the symbol of this Brazil team – a symbol of over-exuberant, brainless defending.

Toni Kroos is congratulated by his teammates after scoring Germany's fourth goal – the scale of the victory is just starting to become apparent.

Mbappé the symbol of a new French revolution

France 4 Croatia 2

15 July 2018 | Moscow | Final

FROM HENRY WINTER, CHIEF FOOTBALL WRITER

What a weekend for the French, with Bastille Day followed by the storming of the Croatian defence. France were not at their fluid best, but Kylian Mbappé, Antoine Griezmann and Paul Pogba ensured an epic final to climax the greatest World Cup since 1982.

At the end, as the heavens opened, Mbappé grasped the World Cup with his left hand, pointed to it with his right, and then very gently planted a kiss on the top. He has been so vital to the French triumph, to the tour de force around Russia, deserving of this wild, immense celebration.

Mbappé and the other French players grabbed Didier Deschamps and gave him the bumps, as Lucas Hernandez ran around the edge, laughing and spraying water at the coach. Deschamps was eventually released and he stood there, smiling at his players, his mind surely going back to when he lifted the trophy 20 years ago. He embraced history, too, yesterday, joining Mario Zagallo and Franz Beckenbauer as the only men to win the World Cup as players and coaches.

The defeated Croatia players stood there, stunned, some like Mario Mandzukic staring ahead as if in a trance. Almost two hours earlier, Croatia's tireless sole striker had conceded the first ever own goal in a World Cup final when Griezmann's free kick skimmed off his head and past Danijel Subasic after 18 minutes. [...]

Croatia were sporting in defeat, going up and shaking [the referee's] hand, knowing that they gave everything. So many times during this glorious tournament, Croatia have shown their character, their fight, coming back from missed penalties, confronting adversity.

Kylian Mbappé, the sensational France forward, clutches the trophy after scoring the final goal in his team's thrilling World Cup final victory over Croatia.

SHOCKS & UPSETS

England's lowest ebb

USA 1 England 0

29 June 1950 | Belo Horizonte
Group 2

A sensation was caused here today when the United States beat England by one goal to none in their Association football match in Pool B of the World Cup. Probably never before has an England team played so badly. The chances they missed were legion. With the American goal at their mercy, the forwards blazed over the bar or hesitated near goal to allow a lively defence to rob them of the ball. At the end the crowd, 20,000 strong, went wild with enthusiasm. Hundreds of spectators rushed to congratulate the jubilant American team as they left the field, and carried the players shoulder high.

The Americans hung stubbornly to the lead they gained after 38 minutes when their centre-forward, Gaetjens, scored with a fine shot from 20 yards into the corner of the net. Yet England had only themselves to blame for defeat. Mortensen skied the ball over the crossbar on several occasions, and he and Bentley had the ball taken off their feet when in good positions near goal. Mannion, too, missed a great opportunity of scoring when he shot too high from an unmarked position in front of goal at the end of half an hour. The small ground and the close marking of the United States defenders seemed to upset the English players in their close passing game, and repeated switches in the forward line during the second half brought no results.

They had some bad luck, it is true, particularly after half-time, but the Americans also went near to increasing their lead on occasions with sudden breaks-away.

England goalkeeper Bert Williams watches in relief as a United States effort drops behind the goal. Goalscorer Joe Gaetjens is on hand just in case.

Jubilant supporters carry off captain Fritz Walter and Horst Eckel after West Germany's stunning victory over the mighty Hungarians.

West Germany stun the magical Magyars

West Germany 3
Hungary 2

4 July 1954 | Berne | Final

FROM GEOFFREY GREEN,
ASSOCIATION FOOTBALL CORRESPONDENT

Germany 3, Hungary 2. In those few words of cold print is enclosed one of the most dramatic and certainly one of the most surprising finals in the whole history of the World Cup. No one, using pure logic, could have foreseen anything but a Hungarian victory. But now in the persistent rain of a day that might have come straight from an English winter a great and simple lesson was taught Nothing is over until the final whistle, and the only certainty of life is its uncertainty. So Germany are the world champions against all the odds and against all premeditated opinion, except, perhaps, that of their excited 20,000-odd supporters who formed perhaps a third – and a vociferous third at that – of the gathering within the Wankdorf Stadium here.

Thus, amidst surging closing scenes, with the waving of Deutschland banners forming a rich backcloth, the precious golden trophy was presented by Mr J. Rimet, the father of the competition, to Walter and his gallant team. At their side stood the Hungarians, gallant also, and generous in defeat though understandably dejected that their first loss in four years of football, which included the Olympic prize, should have come at the very moment when their superb prowess seemed about to be crowned.

Their deportment, let it be said, at this moment was all that it should have been.

It must have been all the more difficult for them to bear, too, for the realisation that they ought to have won must have chilled and prodded them as they stood there at the very end in the slanting rain. Certainly on the run of the play, and on the chances that went spinning away, the victory ought to have been theirs. So easily could they have scored five or six goals in all. At the very last, too, they might have rescued their record that was slipping away, a record that has spanned four triumphant years embracing 28 victories and four draws. For even after Rahn had shot past Groscis for Germany's third and last decisive thrust with only five minutes left, there was Puskas to hit home Toth's diagonal cross from a position behind Posipal, the right back.

The very last minutes were then unwinding themselves. But the flag of Mr Griffiths, the linesman on Puskas's wing, went up for offside, and so the last drop of succour was dashed from their lips. It seemed a doubtful decision, but angles are often difficult from the stand, and one must leave it at that. Yet it is tragic that so much hung on such a decision.

A fairy tale on Teesside

North Korea 1 Italy 0

19 July 1966 | Ayresome Park, Middlesbrough | Group 4

BARRY DAVIES

We came expecting the inevitable. We left having witnessed the impossible – or what had seemed so. For a week now the north-east has longed for a match to remember and at Ayresome Park last night it happened. North Korea wrote a fairy tale into the history of the World Cup. Italy were pushed into limbo.

Now, barring another upset tonight (Chile beating Russia), the little men from the land of the morning calm will take their talents to Goodison Park for a quarter-final match with Portugal. England's defeat at the hands of the United States 16 years ago had nothing on this night of emotion, which left a North Korean commentator with tears streaming down his face as he sent the fantastic news to the Far East.

From the Koreans' first moments on the football fields of this country the inhabitants of Middlesbrough took them to their hearts. Now they cheered the Koreans all the way and, in the end, shared their joy.

The goal, greeted with a noise like thunder, came with three minutes of normal time remaining in the first half. A Korean attack was broken up, the ball half-cleared: and there was little Pak Seung Zin driving it back again with his head for Pak Doo Ik to slam past Albertosi. [...]

The Korean FA President, Kim Kis Soo, said afterwards that the Koreans owed much to the support and encouragement of the Middlesbrough crowd. He added that Korea had prepared well for the World Cup. The team's coach, Myun Rye Hyung, said his team would again display its skill and technique in the quarter-final, but it was impossible to make a prediction. The team had improved with every game here, but the support of the spectators had helped. The players, he said, had lived up to the honour of the fatherland.

The North Korea players and officials can hardly believe it; they have beaten Italy – tipped to win the tournament by Times' correspondent Geoffrey Green – to qualify for the quarter-finals.

Shamed Scotland players ignore their furious fans as they make their way down the tunnel after drawing with rank outsiders Iran.

Ally's Army in full retreat

Iran 1 Scotland 1

7 June 1978 | Córdoba | Group 4

FROM NORMAN FOX, FOOTBALL CORRESPONDENT

Scotland's sad, shame-faced World Cup will surely end when they meet the Netherlands in Mendoza on Sunday when they will have to win by a substantial margin to reach the second round at the expense of the Dutch. In truth they have not won the right to do so and can now be considered beyond hope. Having lost to Peru last Saturday, they faced Iran here tonight without soul and again failed. By various means, they have not brought credit to British football.

This was an even worse performance than against the Peruvians simply because Iran are such outsiders in the world of football. They simply attempted to stop Scotland and so improve their own standing internationally. They not only succeeded in their modest ambitions but gave Scotland their only goal.

One cannot give Scotland a serious chance of scoring the three clear goals which is now the minimum they require on Sunday even though the Dutch were sufficiently below par in their match today to be held to a draw by those bright Peruvians. The Scots are virtually in the departure lounge and they must expect that their homecoming will be a sorrowful affair. It must be said that they had been mismanaged and today their football lacked the spirit of revival that was desperately needed if they were to make even token amends for all the misdemeanours of the past week.

Iran's defensive steel, predictably, was their forte, although the result they achieved was a credit to the sort of determination that Scotland were unable to raise. When they crossed the border into Scotland's half it was usually with only two players, but their organisation was solidly in the cause of self-preservation. [...]

Scotland have had their share of failure in the World Cup, but never before been so humiliated.

Lechkov sends Germany crashing head first

Bulgaria 2 Germany 1

10 July 1994 | New Jersey
Quarter-final

FROM DAVID MILLER

In one of the most notable surprises of the World Cup since Germany themselves defeated Hungary in the 1954 final, the champions were ousted in the quarter-final here in the Giants Stadium yesterday by Bulgaria, the rank outsiders. Until 14 minutes from the end, Germany had looked calm, clear victors.

Then, suddenly, they were toppled by two goals in three minutes, the winning header coming from Yordan Lechkov, who plays with Hamburger SV and whose 27th birthday had been the day before.

It is hard to describe the look of dismay, disbelief and, so unusual for them, capitulation on the faces of the German team in the instant that Lechkov soared above Helmer to meet a looping cross from Yankov. With barely six minutes remaining, the Germans knew that, barring some unlikely stroke of fortune, their dominance that has extended through three final matches since 1982 –twice runners-up – was, for the moment, at an end.

How the Bulgarians, who now play Italy in the semi-finals, relished their triumph, as did those of their supporters billowing their red-white-and-green flags here in this huge stadium. As the Germans dragged themselves dejectedly away from the scene and down the tunnel after the finish, the Bulgarians, the substitutes, the trainers and just about anyone present from Sofia who could get a foot on the pitch staged a photo-session for the benefit of posterity that was worthy of Hollywood. You would think they had won the trophy.

An ecstatic Yordan Lechkov celebrates the brilliant diving header that gave Bulgaria an unlikely quarter-final victory against Germany.

Senegal strike a blow for Africa

Senegal 1 France 0

31 May 2002 | Seoul | Group A

FROM SIMON BARNES

We thought it was all hype, but it was nothing of the kind. The World Cup seemed nothing but overblown and absurd expectation – but it turns out to have been the most cautious and conservative understatement.

For the first match of the competition was as glorious as anything football can produce: skill, melodrama, carpet-chewing tension, the humbling of the world champions, but above all, the greatest gift that football can bring to the world: the victory of the underdog and the overwhelming triumph of hope.

France won the World Cup in 1998, and were the favourites of knowledgable tipsters to win again. But football has a way of making knowledgable tipsters look like twits and world champions like twerps. For France, proud France, were beaten in the opening match by Senegal. Sound the trumpets, sing loud hosannas: it is a result that pleases everybody in the world except the French, and a good few of us can take their disappointment in our stride.

But gloating over the losers is missing the point. It was the victory of the little guys that touched hearts and tore fingernails as the preposterous plot unfolded.

Senegal, in their first World Cup, were happy just to be here – but they also sneakily fancied their chances of making their mark. They won by the only goal of the game, and no goalscorer over the coming four weeks will have a better name. Savour it Papa Bouba Diop. It is a name to go alongside Pak Doo Ik and Roger Milla in great World Cup underdog stories of our time.

Senegal players dance with delight after their victory over holders France that got the 2002 World Cup off to an incredible start.

South Korea shake up the old world order

South Korea 2 Italy 1

18 June 2002 | Daejeon
Second round

FROM KEVIN McCARRA

The man whom Serie A considers disposable has ejected Italy. As Ahn Jung Hwan lay on the ground, his emotionally saturated body reduced to paralysis, he cannot have wondered where he will go after Perugia. Having missed a penalty kick earlier, he had just entered the history and legend of South Korea with the golden goal that felled another of the supposed giants of football at this World Cup.

If this tournament does lack a truly great side, it may be the better for it. There is no nostalgia for the established order of sport when the anarchy makes the pulse race like this. On an ordinary night, Italy would have won. They were ahead, with two minutes left, when a chip from Hwang Sun-hong came at an awkward height to Christian Panucci.

Instead of clearing, he brushed the ball into the path of Seol Ki Hyeon, who buried the chance with a first-time shot.

Then, one sensed the destination that the game would take. South Korea are not to be resisted. That owes a little to the qualities that Guus Hiddink, the coach, has cultivated, but a great deal to the bizarre, inexplicable shape that the greatest of competitions assumes in the month of its life.

Nothing would avail Italy, who had been so organised and sure of themselves for so long. The golden goal might have fallen to them, despite their reduced numbers. Seol Ki-hyeon's misjudged back-heel put Rino Gattuso, a substitute, through, only for his drive to be turned over the crossbar by Lee Woon Jae. With their inspiring support, there always seems to be a riposte from South Korea and Ahn had the last word. Rising to Lee Young Pyo's cross, he headed accurately into the corner of the net.

Ecstasy for South Korea's Ahn Jung Hwan after his header three minutes from the end of extra time completed South Korea's remarkable win over Italy.

Germany lose cloak of invincibility

South Korea 2 Germany 0
27 June 2018 | Kazan | Group F

FROM ALYSON RUDD

It comes to something when you hear Germans tutting at the folly of arrogance but the simmering anger of a nation was reflected among the media here in Kazan. This was one of the all-time World Cup shocks and the fault lies in the coaching staff who failed to notice that anything was wrong before the tournament began.

The four-times champions, who have reached the last eight in 16 consecutive World Cups, failed to even escape the group stage after this defeat by South Korea. It is the first time that Germany have exited in the first stage since 1938 and for those looking through a domestic prism, this is the first time that England have outperformed Germany since 1966.

There will be as much glee in England as there is despair in Germany. The only blot for Gareth Southgate's team is that they cannot face Germany in the knockout stages, for this was a side ripe for being humiliated by confident youngsters.

Joachim Löw had said more than once that his team were vulnerable to swift counterattacks and yet had not addressed the problem. In the pre-tournament friendlies against Austria and Saudi Arabia, his team had been ponderous but Löw said that he had thought that he would be able to change things with the touch of a button, to switch Germany on, to light the fuse that had seen them progress so serenely four years ago. His team had then scored seven past a host nation and had left opponents quivering before a ball was kicked.

Four years on from it being Germany who humiliated Brazil, it was now Germany's turn to feel the pain.

A tearful exit for Thomas Müller after defeat by South Korea means Germany failed to qualify for the later stages of a World Cup for the first time since 1938.

CLASHES & CONTROVERSIES

The battle of Berne

Hungary 4 Brazil 2

27 June 1954 | Berne
Quarter-final

FROM GEOFFREY GREEN,
ASSOCIATION FOOTBALL CORRESPONDENT

In one of the bitterest, fiercest, and tensest matches probably ever fought – that is the correct word – Hungary this evening, in slanting rain within the Wankdorf Stadium here, reached the semi-final for the World Cup with a victory by four goals to two over Brazil.

Here were two of the greatest sides in the world finally destroying their own superb artistry by the barefaced and attempted annihilation of each other by unethical tactics. Never in my life have I seen such cruel tackling, the cutting down of opponents as if with a scythe, followed by threatening attitudes and sly jabs when officialdom was engaged elsewhere.

In the course of it all N. Santos, the Brazilian left-back, and Bozsik, Hungary's captain at right-half in the absence of the injured Puskas, were sent off the field some 20 minutes from the end, and in the dying moments Humberto, the Brazilian inside-right, also was dispatched to the dressing room by Mr Ellis, the English referee. By this time Hungary, long since reduced in strength by an injury also to J. Toth before half-time, had won a deserved tactical victory with

their fourth and decisive goal three minutes from the end.

At the end a minor revolution broke out. First it began on the field between spectators, photographers, police, and a general swarming melee of bodies. After the teams had struggled into the tunnel out of sight under the stand, more trouble broke out. Whom it concerned in particular could only be left to the imagination, as more police were summoned up and disappeared from view down that same tunnel.

Let it be said at once that it was the Brazilians who began all the trouble. In the very first minutes Hidegkuti had the right leg of his trousers torn away as he was held back. It took the Hungarians a long time to be goaded into retaliation, for this one suspects is not their approach to football. And all the while, as the fires simmered and finally flared up, it was they who were trying to play the more considered, cultured game along the ground. Praise be this was not the final, and so far as world domination of the game is concerned if this is what it breeds then the British Isles are well out of it.

Swiss police had to get involved at the end of the game as fights broke out between players and officials – and continued in the tunnel.

The battle of Santiago

Chile 2 Italy 0

2 June 1962 | Santiago
Group 2

I n *The Times*, Geoffrey Green made do with the word "tempestuous", and that was in a single paragraph rounding up the day's other action at the end of his report of England's 3-1 win over Argentina. But when the film of the match was shown by BBC television a few days later, David Coleman did not mince his words. "Good evening," he greeted viewers. "The game you are about to see is the most stupid, appalling, disgusting, and disgraceful exhibition of football possibly in the history of the game." He put the blame for the bloodbath solely on Italy. "If the World Cup is going to survive in its present form something has got to be done about teams that play like this," he continued. The bare facts were that English referee Ken Aston sent off Italy's Giorgio Ferrini and Mario David during Chile's 2-0 win that took them into the quarter-finals of their home World Cup. But the brutality of some of the exchanges went well beyond a normal rough-house match: parts of the action resembled nothing so much as a street brawl. In particular, Chile's Leonel Sánchez laid out David with a left hook that would not have been out of place at Madison Square Garden. Somehow, he stayed on the field.

RICHARD WHITEHEAD

Ken Aston orders off Italy midfielder Giorgio Ferrini after only eight minutes of one of the stormiest matches in history. It needed Chilean police to get him off the pitch.

Rattin brings Wembley to a standstill

England 1 Argentina 0

23 July 1966 | Wembley
Stadium, London | Quarter-final

BY GEOFFREY GREEN, FOOTBALL CORRESPONDENT

England, still without a goal conceded, reached the semi-final round of the World Cup for the first time at Wembley on Saturday, when they beat Argentina, one of the opponents they had feared most.

But if England won narrowly, football itself lost widely. As a match it was like a crumpled, unmade bed. The 88,000 crowd hooted and booed, cheered and laughed in succession as the travesty of pushing, jostling, chopping, holding and tripping unwound. In all this some of the England players themselves were not entirely blameless – conceding perhaps as many free kicks as the Argentines before half-time.

But from the first move, when Peters was obstructed by a flagrant body check, Moore and his men found themselves under provocation. As it was, an afternoon of brilliant sunshine that was draped in black came to a merciful end without the need of extra time and the possible drawing of lots that at one stage seemed certain. [...]

For the rest, it was a mixture of cold comfort farm, stormy weather, and the Keystone Cops. As danders rose there came the "bookings" of Rattin, Artime, and Solari, later joined by Ferreiro and Perfumo, and the brothers Charlton for England.

The flashpoint was reached 10 minutes from the interval. Suddenly it was seen that Rattin, far from the actual play at that moment but adjacent to the German referee, was being ordered off the field. For the next seven minutes there was bedlam. Players and officials jostled on the field, at one moment it seemed the whole Argentina side was about to march off, with the angry threat of fisticuffs close to the surface.

All the while the Wembley crowd kept their good humour remarkably well. Thousands of pounds had been expended on a farce. Yet, in spite of the new squeeze on their pockets, they roared "England! England!" and cheerfully chanted "Why are we waiting?" If it had not been sad, it would have been as funny as some Crazy Gang show.

Chaos at Wembley as police come on to the field to protect West German referee Rudolf Kreitlein from furious Argentina players.

Referee sends for the boys in blue

West Germany 4
Uruguay 0

23 July 1966 | Hillsborough, Sheffield | Quarter-final

GERALD SINSTADT

Mr J Finney, the well-known English referee, with a supporting cast of West German footballers, a diminishing number of Uruguayans, and sundry coaches, trainers and policemen, staged an afternoon of ripe melodrama at Sheffield. For those whose tastes are mainly theatrical it was probably satisfying enough.

On a black day for South America, the Uruguayans contributed wilfully to their own downfall. In five minutes of indiscipline early in the second half, they abandoned any claim to sympathy from spectators and all hope of survival to the semi-finals.

First, a linesman drew the attention of Mr Finney to the prostrate figure of Emmerich. After a brief consultation, Mr Finney pointed and Troche, the Uruguayan captain, departed. He was soon followed, though with great reluctance and a certain amount of police persuasion, by Silva, who had just felled Haller.

The remaining half hour was a travesty. Although Perez, Cortes and Ubinas mounted periodic attacks, most of their colleagues lost heart and, eventually, interest.

Referee Jim Finney had to call for the assistance of the local constabulary after Hector Silva, the Uruguay No.19, refused to leave the field after being sent off.

A stitch-up in Spain

West Germany 1
Austria 0

25 June 1982 | Gijón | Group 2

They called it "the disgrace of Gijón" and the sense of grievance and injustice lingered on for decades in Algeria. Only the Austrians, West Germans and, crucially, FIFA shrugged their shoulders. What happened was this. Austria and West Germany arrived at their final match in Group 2 of the 1982 tournament knowing that a 1-0 win for the Germans would be enough for both teams to progress to the second round. That situation had emerged largely because of some remarkable performances by the unfancied Algerians. In their first game they had delivered one of the tournament's greatest upsets by beating West Germany 2-1. They then lost to Austria but beat Chile 3-2 to be on the cusp of becoming the first African team to qualify for the second phase of the World Cup. The one result they could not afford was a 1-0 win for West Germany.

Horst Hrubesch gave the Germans the early goal they wanted but after that, first to the astonishment and later the fury of the crowd, both teams stopped trying to score. When the game was examined by modern analysts it was revealed that there were only three shots – none of them on target – in the second half and West Germany made only eight tackles. On the terraces, outraged Algerian fans waved banknotes while one German fan set his country's flag alight. An Austrian TV commentator urged viewers to switch off. Despite the worldwide condemnation, the governing body ruled there was nothing they could do. It did lead, however, to an overdue change – the decisive group matches would henceforth be played simultaneously.

RICHARD WHITEHEAD

Furious Algerian fans hold up Spanish banknotes to make it clear what they think of the 'fix' between Austria and West Germany.

Schumacher's place in infamy

West Germany 3 France 3
(West Germany won 5-4 on penalties)
8 July 1982 | Seville | Semi-final

It was not until viewing the slow-motion replays that the full horror of Harald Schumacher's assault on Patrick Battiston became clear. In real time, the eye tended to follow the ball as it rolled wide of the West German post – that was referee Charles Corver's excuse anyway for missing one of the worst, perhaps *the* worst, foul in World Cup history. A thrilling France-West Germany semi-final in Seville was tied at 1-1 when Michel Platini played a typically perceptive crossfield pass to where Battiston, who had only been on the field for ten minutes, was racing into a gaping hole in the middle of the German defence. Schumacher rushed out to meet him on the edge of the penalty area and, seconds after Battiston made contact with the ball, flung his full body weight into the French player. It quickly became apparent that something was seriously wrong. Battiston had cracked ribs, damaged vertebrae, had lost several teeth and was unconscious for half an hour, drifting on the edge of a coma. It took a scandalous seven minutes to find a stretcher and get the stricken player off the field. What shocked the world as much as the injuries was Schumacher's apparent indifference to what he had done. The West Germany goalkeeper merely stood waiting to take the goal kick, his demeanour suggesting he was irritated by the delay. He confirmed his anti-hero status by saving two penalties in the shoot-out which the Germans won 5-4. But the controversy reached such a pitch that messages were exchanged between the two countries' political leaders, Helmut Schmidt and François Mitterrand.

RICHARD WHITEHEAD

Harald Schumacher turns his body and hurls himself at Patrick Battiston a fraction of a second after the French substitute has sent a shot wide of the post.

The Hand of God

Argentina 2 England 1

22 June 1986 | Mexico City
Quarter-final

FROM STUART JONES, FOOTBALL CORRESPONDENT

England yesterday suffered at the hands of the best player in the world. After being nudged out of the quarter-finals in the Aztec Stadium here, Shilton led a posse of players who surrounded the Tunisian referee to complain angrily about the legitimacy of the crucial opening goal. The television cameras supported their claim.

A slow motion replay confirmed that Maradona had indeed used his forearm to put Argentina ahead in the 50th minute. It seemed impossible, anyway, that he could have extended his stocky frame that measures only 5ft 4in to outjump Shilton, complete his exchange with Valdano and shake the foundations of England's World Cup challenge.

Yet if justice was to play a cruel role in their eventual downfall, there can be little doubt that they were beaten by a superior side.

FROM DAVID MILLER

A last word on Maradona's handling. I do not condone his cheating, though I am by no means convinced that his handling was intentional in the moment he outjumped Shilton. That he did not own up to the referee on the spot is hardly surprising. We cannot expect Maradona to be some Corinthian symbol of probity in a sport in which every player is at some time cheating, not excluding the English. As I have said before, Maradona has been infinitely more cheated against in his career than he has himself been a cheat.

Diego Maradona jumps with England goalkeeper Peter Shilton and clearly uses his hand to guide the ball over his head into the net, sparking a controversy which carried on until the Argentinian's death in 2020.

An ugly spat in the San Siro

West Germany 2
Netherlands 1

24 June 1990 | Milan
Second round

FROM DAVID MILLER

To say that these two teams do not like each other would be one of the understatements of sport. The worst aspects of the match served to mar an evening of otherwise breathtaking incidents and action. Midway through the first half, Völler, of Germany, and Rijkaard, of the Netherlands, were sent off together for vulgar rowdyism by Loustau, an Argentinian referee, who gave an exemplary performance in a tortuously difficult match. [...]

The sendings-off followed an initial and severe foul by Rijkaard, who heavily brought down Völler. A free kick was given but Völler was booked for dissent. Almost immediately, van Breukelen, in the Dutch goal had to deal with a harmless high ball. Völler, coming in, jumped and made only incidental contact with van Breukelen, seeming to have no intention of charging him illegally. Völler fell, Rijkaard came up and started gesticulating, and after pushing and shoving and some spitting by Rijkaard, the pair were despatched to the dressing room like a couple of cats.

Frank Rijkaard of the Netherlands is about to spit at West Germany's Rudi Völler after both had been sent off in a fractious second-round encounter.

The final disgrace

West Germany 1
Argentina 0

8 July 1990 | Rome | Final

FROM DAVID MILLER

Once again Argentina has demeaned football. The deplorable World Cup final of 1990 will be remembered not for the way West Germany won it, mechanically and without style, but the manner in which Argentina lost it, disgracefully.

The nation which has so much to give the game in skill, winners in 1978 and 1986, now wore the sour, petulant face which we have also too often witnessed in the past. The only good thing that could be said about the match is that Brehme's penalty eight minutes from the end ensured that Argentina lost and that the watching sporting world would not have to endure more extra time or a penalty lottery.

This was the worst final ever played, worse than the first hour of 1982 between Germany and Italy, and the first in which anyone was sent off, Monzon and Dezotti, of Argentina, being dismissed by Codesal, the Mexican referee, who gave an alarmingly erratic performance. Codesal had missed the clearest of penalties against Argentina's goalkeeper, Goycoechea, after an hour, and when he sent off Dezotti a few minutes from the end for manhandling Kohler, the German defender, Codesal should have dismissed him too for blatant time-wasting.

In Argentina's seven matches during the past four weeks, there have been eight players sent off: three of their own and five opponents. It is symptomatic of their performances that for the final they were missing four suspended players, Caniggia, Olarticoechea, Giusti and Batista. After the final whistle, the rugged Batista had to be restrained from molesting the referee.

As in 1966, following their display of wanton fouling against England in the quarter-final, Argentina should be censured by FIFA and severely fined. In front of billions of television viewers they have given an appalling example of the game.

Referee Edgardo Codesal shows the red card to Gustavo Dezotti while Pedro Troglio protests. The 1990 final was a night of shame for Argentina – and the tournament.

Wayne Rooney's red mist

Portugal 0 England 0

(Portugal won 3-1 on penalties)
1 July 2006 | Gelsenkirchen
Quarter-final

FROM SIMON BARNES, CHIEF SPORTS WRITER

This has been Wayne's World. From beginning to bitter, bitter end, this World Cup has been Wayne Rooney's story. A story of wild hope that became a story of despair; a story of compelling talents that became a story of spectacular flaws; a story of the search for the ultimate prize that now becomes a story of a search for redemption.

Sven-Göran Eriksson has always been vilified for his caution, but at the end it was his one great gamble that undid him. Eriksson picked Rooney for England before he was a first-team regular for Everton and as Rooney lit up the European Championship in Portugal two years ago, it seemed, it really seemed that England would go into the World Cup as serious contenders. With a fit and firing Rooney, anything was possible.

But Rooney brought England down on Saturday. How the patterns repeat themselves: the sending-off, the wild courage of the survivors, the penalties, the tears. And only four years before we must do it all again. We might just have recovered by then.

So much fuss about a 20-year-old boy with a talent for rough and tumble and bit of a temper on him. But if we value football, we must value people such as Rooney and appreciate the way that he teaches us that our greatest strengths are always, always our greatest weaknesses. This is a simple enough principle, but sport showcases it better than anything else on earth. It is, you might say, the guiding principle of sport and it was demonstrated to perfection on Saturday.

Rooney's talent is for the maelstrom of sport, for the *Sturm und Drang* – storm and stress – of football. He is at his best in contact, in the collision of desperate bodies, in situations in which his strengths and his strength of will come to the fore.

After a midfield tussle which ends with both players on the ground, Wayne Rooney appears to stamp on Carvalho's thigh.

Rooney sees red and England's hopes of beating Portugal in the World Cup quarter-final go with him.

Zidane's shameful exit

Italy 1 France 1

(Italy won 5-3 on penalties)
9 July 2006 | Berlin | Final

FROM MATT DICKINSON,
CHIEF FOOTBALL CORRESPONDENT

A vision persuaded Zinedine Zidane to come out of international retirement and something unexplained in his head propelled him back there last night, the France captain leaving football with an indelible stain across his reputation unless the next few days of inquest can uncover evidence that he was the victim of intolerable, verbal provocation.

If not, the 18th World Cup final will for ever be associated with the sad, shameful end of a great footballer as much as Italy's triumph in adversity. Marcello Lippi's men paraded their trophy in the Olympic Stadium last night under a downpour of silver glitter but the mind kept drifting to the mental state and the whereabouts of Zidane; banned from returning to the pitch to collect his loser's medal after his dismissal for a violent headbutt.

He had opened the scoring with an uncharacteristically cocky, dinked penalty but, as acts of self-indulgence go, that had nothing on his rhino's thrust into the chest of Marco Materazzi with ten minutes of extra time remaining.

Had the big defender said something that insulting? Or was there something else eating away at Zidane as he counted down the final minutes of his playing career? As this final was settled by shoot-out – Fabio Grosso completing Italy's perfect set – and his team condemned to defeat while their leader sat in the dressing room, the prospect of a lifetime of regrets surely overcame him.

Such a petulant end was all the more difficult to explain because France had dominated this final and were still doing so when Zidane departed. He will never know whether the outcome might have been different had he only stayed on the field, but his departure was bound to sap the spirit of his team-mates.

His career has not been without its moments of spite (he was also sent off during the 1998 finals for a stamp), but he had shown no signs of breakdown in this match. He had brought a brilliant save from Gianluigi Buffon in extra time and, on every measurable scale of football dominance, France could claim a moral victory until their captain's sensational exit.

Zidane is forced to walk past the trophy he could have been lifting after his sensational sending-off.

England cross after line call

Germany 4 England 1

27 June 2010 | Bloemfontein
Second round

To the Germans it felt like long overdue reparation for Geoff Hurst's second goal in the 1966 World Cup final. But England's players, management and fans were in no mood for a history lesson after their exit from the 2010 tournament in South Africa came after another row about whether the ball had crossed the goalline. The difference was that this time it was not even close. England had been 2-0 down in the last-16 tie in Bloemfontein before Matthew Upson pulled a goal back after 36 minutes. Almost immediately England attacked again and Frank Lampard struck a lofted shot from the edge of the area that beat Manuel Neuer, hit the bar and bounced down at least a yard over the line. But referee Jorge Larrionda waved play on and assistant Mauricio Espinosa kept his flag down. "It is incredible that there is no [video] technology," fumed England manager Fabio Capello. "We played with five referees and they cannot decide whether it is a goal or not. That one goal would have made the game completely different." Lampard agreed. "I think we have to have technology," he said. "Before the World Cup we were told about a million different rule changes that hardly affect the game. And the big one, that affects the game, hasn't been brought in. It is a no-brainer." The row tended to obscure the fact that Germany went on to record a clear 4-1 victory. "It is the English custom at these times to seek someone to blame," wrote Simon Barnes in *The Times*. The incident had one lasting benefit – it prompted FIFA to shift its Luddite stance on technology.

RICHARD WHITEHEAD

The evidence looks clear enough as Frank Lampard's shot bounces down behind Manuel Neuer but the officials ruled no goal and England were denied an equaliser.

Luis Suárez becomes the biter bit

Uruguay 1 Italy 0

24 June 2014 | São Paulo
Group D

Just when you thought football had lost its capacity to shock, along came the Liverpool and Uruguay striker Luis Suárez. In his country's final Group D match against Italy in São Paulo, Suárez was involved in some off-the-ball penalty area jostling with the Italy defender Giorgio Chiellini. Nothing unusual in that; Suárez's game was built on aggression as much as the power and quality of his finishing. Both players went down in the penalty area, Chiellini in apparent agony, Suárez holding his mouth. Only after seeing slow-motion replays did it become clear what had happened – Suárez had sunk his teeth into his opponent's shoulder. The Italian pulled the collar of his shirt down to show the wound but referee Marco Rodríguez had seen nothing and could take no action. But there was no getting away with it for Suárez, who had committed two previous biting offences, one while playing for Liverpool. Two days later, FIFA banned him for nine international matches, and from all forms of the game for four months.

RICHARD WHITEHEAD

An enraged Giorgio Chiellini points out what has happened to the referee, who had not seen the incident, while Suárez claims to be hurt himself.

ON THE SPOT

O'Leary starts green party

Ireland 0 Romania 0

(Ireland win 5-4 on penalties)
25 June 1990 | Genoa
Second round

FROM CLIVE WHITE

It was inevitable that a side that can grind out draws like nobody else should take this second-round match through full time and extra time, without a goal being scored or conceded, to its ultimate penalty shoot-out conclusion.

Even then, the Republic maintained a status quo until 4-4, when Timofte, a Romanian substitute, shaped to shoot in such a way that it was obvious to everyone within the Luigi Ferarris stadium, and notably to Bonner, the Irish goalkeeper, that he would strike the ball to Bonner's right. He did, and Bonner saved, as one would expect him to.

As so often in these cruel situations, it was not so much an heroic deed as a terribly sad misdeed.

A more desperate figure than Timofte, it was difficult to imagine, standing there, yanking up both sides of his shorts in a fit of horror at his dreadful act and its consequences.

If there had to be a hero, it was the popular O'Leary, who, under the burden of great expectation, converted the following penalty as a hush descended on the vast stadium. For O'Leary, it was a moment worth waiting for, after finally joining in the World Cup action in the third minute of extra time as substitute for Staunton. The entire Irish team and staff converged upon him as though he had just won the World Cup itself. Indeed, this may have been their final, though I for one would not like to bet against it.

Joy for David O'Leary. Forced into international exile in Jack Charlton's regime, he came on as a substitute and coolly converted the shoot-out winner.

Maradona shatters a nation's dream

Argentina 1 Italy 1

(Argentina won 4-3 on penalties)
3 July 1990 | Naples
Semi-final

FROM RODDY FORSYTH

Italy's grand vision of winning the World Cup in Rome on Sunday was shattered last night when they were beaten in the semi-final by Argentina in the cruel drama of a penalty shoot-out. The expectations of a nation were extinguished as Donadoni and Serena had their penalties saved, while Maradona, playing in his adopted Naples home, arrogantly placed and converted what proved to be the winning kick.

If Maradona, restored to the peak of his form, was the architect of a stirring performance by the World Cup holders, the deciding factor was the ability of Goycochea, the Argentinian goalkeeper, to anticipate the direction of Donadoni and Serena's kicks – both of which he reached with two-handed saves after diving to his left.

The match, though unfailingly absorbing, was not, however, a credit to the sport or to Argentina's disciplinary record. Four of their players, Ruggeri, Caniggia, Olarticoechea and Batista were cautioned, while Giusti, who had earlier been booked, was shown the red card in extra time after an incident off the ball left Baggio sprawling on the turf.

If it was always likely that this contest would prove volatile in the heat and humidity of Naples, what could not have been forseen was Argentina's resilience, both in retrieving their position after Schillaci's opening goal and in the manner of their transformation from the self-pitying side of previous rounds into one determined not to surrender its crown. [...]

Even with Argentina reduced to ten men, Italy could not impose themselves and so it went to penalty kicks. For Argentina, it was the second time in five days that a match was to be settled in this fashion.

The first six attempts were successful, with Baresi, Baggio and De Agostini scoring for Italy while Serrizuela, Burruchaga and Olarticoechea kept Argentina level. Then came Goycoechea's denial of Donadoni and Serena.

A wretched groan arose from all sides of the stadium as the Italian contingent saw their country's most cherished dream dashed. It was also the signal for wild, almost hysterical celebration by the Argentinians.

In the stadium where he was worshipped for his exploits with Naples, Diego Maradona cooly converts the decisive penalty in Argentina's shoot-out victory over hosts Italy.

England bow out in the cruellest fashion

England 1 West Germany 1

(West Germany win 4-3 on penalties)
4 July 1990 | Turin | Semi-final

FROM STUART JONES, FOOTBALL CORRESPONDENT

A dream which almost became reality last night turned into a personal nightmare for Stuart Pearce and Chris Waddle. The unfortunate pair will forever be haunted by the dreadful moment they missed the penalties which condemned England to the role of runners-up in a dazzling and ultimately cruel World Cup semi-final here.

They and their colleagues deserved a kinder fate. They had outplayed "the most impressive team in the tournament", as Bobby Robson had justifiably described West Germany, to an astonishing degree in the first 40 minutes. They had recovered from Brehme's goal, the result of a wicked deflection, to equalise through Lineker with only ten minutes left in normal time.

Pushed into extra-time for the third successive match, they called on the spirit which had lifted them beyond reasonable expectations and struck a post through Waddle. The Germans also struck an upright through Buchwald before the second semi-final, like the first in Naples on Tuesday night, became a game of Russian roulette.

Lineker, Beardsley, and, less convincingly, Platt all scored but Pearce's penalty cannoned off the legs of the German goalkeeper, Illgner, and Waddle, with the destiny of the tie at his trembling feet, hit his high over the bar. Thus, the Germans go into their third successive World Cup final and against Argentina, their conquerors in Mexico City four years ago.

Chris Waddle's penalty sails over the bar to end England's dream of reaching the final and conclude a night of high drama in Turin.

Baggio finds the clear blue sky over LA

Brazil 0 Italy 0

(Brazil win 3-2 on penalties)
17 July 1994 | Los Angeles | Final

FROM DAVID MILLER

Justice, of the most unsatisfactory kind, was finally done. Brazil, consistently the most attacking team of the fifteenth World Cup finals and of the ultimate match against Italy, became the first to win the trophy on a penalty shoot-out. They thus became the first four-time winners.

There is no more wretched conclusion to a great match than this, but the truth is that Brazil had been dominant throughout much of 120 minutes. [...]

The renowned defensive qualities of Italy enabled them to survive for two hours, their attack blunted by the evident injury to Roberto Baggio. It was ironic that the last kick of the match, Baggio's miss on Italy's fifth penalty kick, giving Brazil a 3-2 advantage, should have decided the destiny of the cup. It was the most ill-judged decision, to allow Roberto Baggio to take a penalty, for with a hamstring injury it is not possible to pull the foot back properly for the striking blow.

Roberto Baggio stands all alone against the stunning backdrop of the Rose Bowl, as Brazil begin their celebrations.

Beckham's shot at redemption

England 1 Argentina 0
7 June 2002 | Sapporo | Group F

FROM SIMON BARNES, CHIEF SPORTS WRITER

The past is done, it can never be changed. No harm can ever be undone, no folly can ever be made wise again, no deed, good or evil, can ever be called back. Time just doesn't have a reverse gear. But try telling David Beckham that. He has been at war with the past for four solid years – and last night he won.

Four years ago his act of idiotic irresponsibility caused England to be knocked out of the World Cup by Argentina. Yesterday it was his highly developed sense of responsibility that revived England's World Cup ambitions when it seemed that all hope had gone. In a match against Argentina – who else? The wheel has turned full circle.

Leadership. Calm. Maturity. Responsibility. All the words that could never have been applied to Beckham four years ago have been raining down on him for months. You can tell a great sportsman not merely by his skill, but by the way he deals with an occasion. There are flat-track bullies who rise to the small occasion. And there are people like Beckham. Yesterday was the most massive occasion of his life. And he rose.

Do I make too much of a penalty? No I do not. The penalty was merely the last point of a story that has enthralled us all for four years, the story of the decline and rise of David Beckham. Against any opponents it would have been something to savour: but against Argentina...

With a typically sweet strike of the ball, David Beckham drives his penalty straight down the middle of the goal and past Argentina goalkeeper Pablo Cavallero.

England shot out again

Portugal 0 England 0

(Portugal win 3-1 on penalties)
1 July 2006 | Gelsenkirchen
Quarter-finals

MATTHEW SYED

Anyone who says that penalties are a lottery are deluding themselves. Let me give you some statistics (if you can bear to read them).

In World Cup finals matches, Germany have taken part in four penalty shoot-outs and won all of them, nailing 17 out of 18 strikes. England, on the other hand, have played three, lost three. You do not need a PhD in maths to see that this is not a distribution that could credibly be described as random.

Besides, we have the evidence of what happened on the pitch. Last week, the Germans raced in and struck the ball with the clean, crisp fluency that you would expect from men who insure their feet for millions. The penalties of the England players on Saturday, on the other hand, had all the conviction of a David Cameron press release.

To get a handle on what might be at issue, let us take a detour to the training pitch. Ask any professional player and he will tell you that he invariably scores penalties in practice, which is hardly surprising when you consider that the ball is struck from 12 yards at a velocity of up to 70mph at a target area of more than 21 square yards.

The difference, then, between Germany and England is not to be found in their respective abilities.

No, the difference is to be found in what happens between the players' ears when they step up to the plate in the crucible of a World Cup showdown. The Germans are able to replicate what they do in practice every week of the year. The English are not. That is the whole 12 yards.

The inescapable conclusion is that the England football team suffer from institutionalised choking when it comes to World Cup shoot-outs.

Delight for Portugal, utter dejection for England as another World Cup shoot-out goes against them.

Zidane has chips with everything

Italy 1 France 1

(Italy won 5-3 on penalties)
9 July 2006 | Berlin | Final

FROM MATT DICKINSON,
CHIEF FOOTBALL CORRESPONDENT

Up stepped Zidane and no one could quite believe what the French maestro tried next. Instead of following his familiar short run with a shot whipped into the bottom corner, Zidane, incredibly, went for the floated chip. It is a method known by the cognoscenti as the Panenka after the man who scored the winning spot-kick in the European Championship final of 1976 but, had it been just inches higher, this one would have gone down as a Crouch. With Buffon down on the ground, the ball struck the underside of the bar and bounced a foot over the line. No one seemed sure whether to celebrate or laugh. The greatest player of his generation was fractions away from looking its greatest idiot – a fate that still awaited him.

Softly does it: Zinedine Zidane's chipped Panenka penalty gave France an early lead in the 2006 World Cup final, but almost left him looking foolish.

And finally, England win a shoot-out

England 1 Colombia 1

(England win 4-3 on penalties)
3 July 2018 | Moscow
Second round

FROM HENRY WINTER, CHIEF FOOTBALL WRITER

Whatever Jordan Pickford achieves in his life he will be revered for one vital save here. Whatever Eric Dier does in his career, he will be cherished for one cool, calm kick. Whatever happens with England now, they will always have Moscow. If they continue to play with this resolve, holding their nerve in that brutal test from 12 yards when they have previously folded, England may even return to Moscow.

England supporters keep singing about reaching the final but they next face an obdurate Sweden, far cleaner opponents than the niggling, provocative Colombians, but no less a threat because of their energy, teamwork, athleticism and belief. Yet what last night demonstrated was the confidence that England have, the strengthened mettle that allowed them to achieve what only one England team had done before – win a competitive shoot-out.

England's road map around Europe is scarred with crashes, from penalty defeats in Turin, to London (although Terry Venables's side did win one, against Spain, at Wembley), to Saint-Étienne, to Lisbon, to Gelsenkirchen, to Kiev, but last night it was Moscow, it was Pickford's moment after so much excessive criticism about Adnan Januzaj's goal for Belgium. Pickford's performance was worthy of a Fabergé Egg rather than a Cadbury's Creme Egg.

It was Dier's moment, too, as his introduction for Dele Alii after 81 minutes invited Colombia on and certainly invited controversy.

If the focus and praise picked out Pickford, and then Dier, it settled fully, fondly, deservedly on Gareth Southgate. He had called on his players to "write their own story" here, etching their names in the history books by seizing the moment, but really this was Southgate's story.

This was about penalties, about a man living for 22 years with the painful memory of missing his kick after volunteering in the shoot-out against Germany at Euro 96. Southgate endured all the abuse, the jibes and sarcastic looks from passers-by, horrific for an honourable man who tries to look for the best in people but too often encountered the worst. He showed his players a video of his errant penalty, trying to make light of it, and also making them appreciate that he went "into the darkness" and that they needed to prepare intensely for penalties.

Goalkeeper Jordan Pickford emerged as the hero of England's nerve-shredding penalties win over Colombia.

HEROES

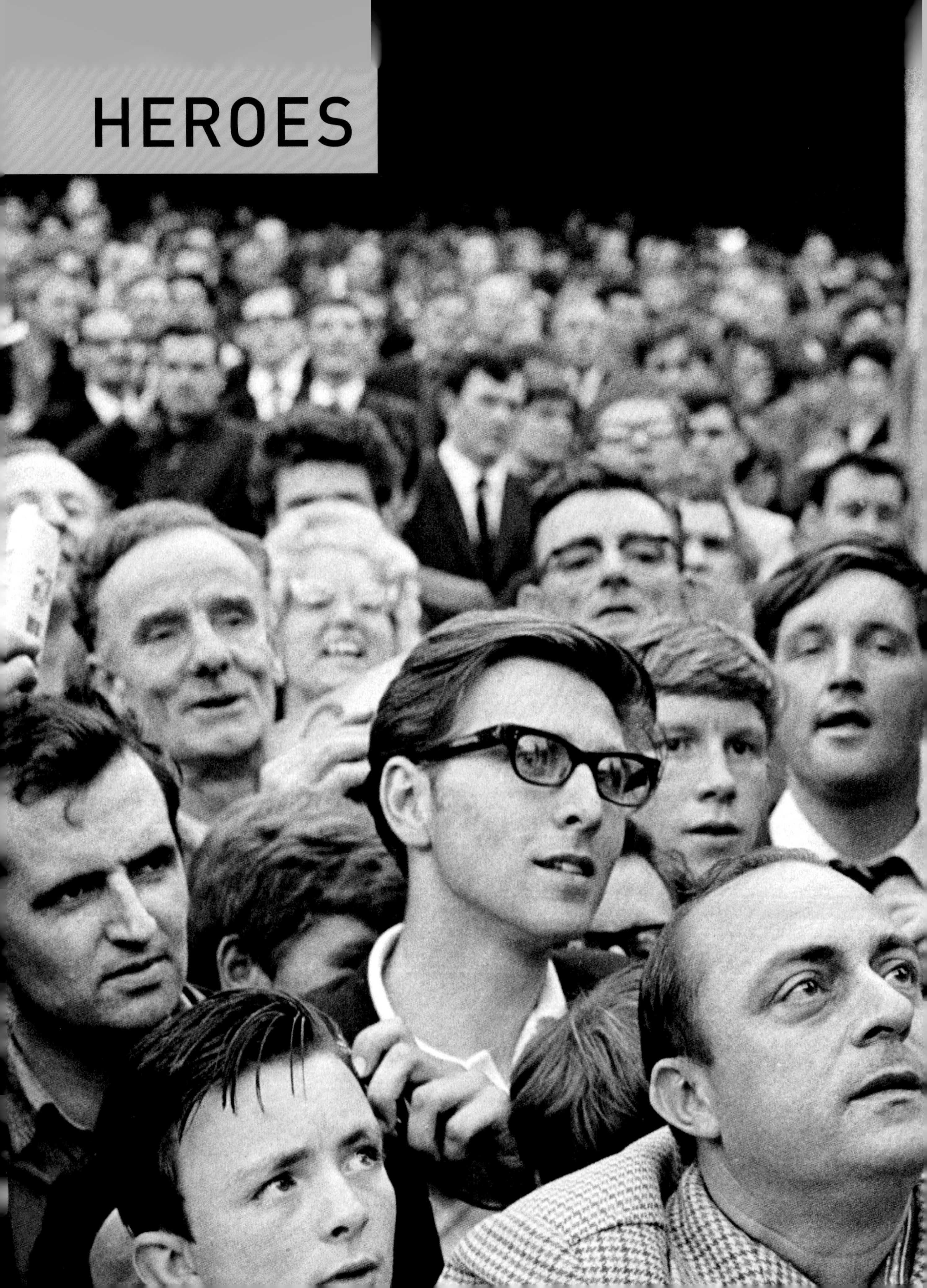

Garrincha

Brazil 3 England 1

10 June 1962 | Viña del Mar
Quarter-final

Garrincha prowled the right wing for Brazil in three World Cups but his finest hour came in 1962 when, with Pelé injured early in the campaign, he took over the mantle of chief creator and goalscorer. His talents were never better demonstrated than in the quarter-final against England. Ray Wilson, the hard-pressed left-back, worked tirelessly to suppress his threat, often helped by Bobby Charlton or Ron Flowers as England doubled up on the winger. Remarkably, given that he was one of the smallest players on the field, he scored the opener with a powerful header from Mario Zagallo's corner. Gerry Hitchens equalised before half-time but Brazil retook the lead when Ron Springett could not hold Garrincha's free kick and Vavá headed home the

rebound. Just before the hour came Garrincha's pièce de résistance. After wandering in the middle to escape Wilson's terrier-like attentions, he picked up possession some 25 yards out and curled a stunning drive into the top right-hand corner of the net. "For perception, imagination and execution, this was a beautiful goal," wrote Bob Ferrier in *The Times*. Four years earlier in Sweden, Geoffrey Green had paid him the ultimate compliment of comparing him to England's greatest No.7 Stanley Matthews. "There was the shambling walk inviting the tackle as the ball is taken into the back as close as a matador draws in the bull: the feint inwards, and the flick past the defender's left side."

RICHARD WHITEHEAD

England left-back Ray Wilson did an outstanding job in attempting to subdue the threat of Garrincha, but here he fails to stop the Brazilian maestro getting in a cross.

Eusébio

Portugal 5 North Korea 3

23 July 1966 | Goodison Park, Liverpool | Quarter-final

TOM GERMAN

Eusébio; one word, one name is enough to explain Portugal's climb from the trough of adversity to tomorrow night's semi-final against England at Wembley. Adversity stings no more sharply or incredibly than it did at Goodison Park, Liverpool, on Saturday; to concede three goals to the unsung North Koreans in the span of the first 25 minutes was a severe enough wound to drain even the favourites of their spirit and reserves.

To their credit, even though so deeply in trouble, Portugal looked as unconcerned as the moment they stepped out: yet it was Eusébio alone, with his sixth sense for popping up exactly where he is most needed, and his immense flair for seizing the fleeting chance, who finally restored their fortunes.

Simões, roaming busily on either wing, and the hardworking Torres, and Augusto did their share in building Portugal's reply, but one always had the lingering feeling that without Eusébio it would not have been eloquent enough to surmount such a staggering setback. Indeed, he who can contain him at Wembley tomorrow could well earn England a place in the final. [...]

Portugal maintained their measured tread in spite of this amazing situation. Then Eusébio took a hand in affairs: he gave an opponent several yards start and still managed to nip past him to stab home a pass from Augusto, and when Torres was tripped from behind as he manoeuvred to shoot Eusébio demonstrated how penalties should be taken.

The message was now clearly inscribed for all to see: Eusébio's elusive brilliance was hoisting Portugal's challenge and at the same time pressing the Koreans into hurried clearances. When he accepted and swept in Simões's pass on the run in the 57th minute to bring the scores level no one doubted the final outcome. Eusébio waltzed his way through a couple of minutes later, to be felled at the second attempt in the penalty area: the kick, a mere formality, gave him his fourth of the match.

Eusébio is sent flying by a North Korea defender but he got up to score from the penalty spot for his fourth goal of an extraordinary afternoon.

Geoff Hurst

England 4
West Germany 2

30 July 1966
Wembley Stadium, London
Final

RIGHT: *Hurst is joined by his wife Judith as he catches up with Brian Glanville's match report in* The Sunday Times.

BELOW: *Hurst and his West Ham teammate Martin Peters (far right), destined to be England's scorers in the final, share a quiet moment at training.*

So central is Geoff Hurst to the myths and legends of England's World Cup victory in 1966 that it comes as a surprise to be reminded that he had made just five international appearances before the tournament (scoring one goal), was not in the team at the start of the competition, and may never have played at all but for an injury to Jimmy Greaves. As late as the morning of the match, Geoffrey Green in *The Times* was speculating that England manager Alf Ramsey might recall Greaves, who had missed the quarter- and semi-final. Hurst certainly made the most of the opportunity handed to him by Ramsey, scoring the only hat-trick in the history of the final. Not just any old hat-trick either; a header, a right-foot shot and a left-foot shot – the perfect treble. His life would never be the same again, although celebrity took a little while to arrive. On the day after England's 4-2 victory over West Germany, he went home and mowed the lawn.

RICHARD WHITEHEAD

Gerd Müller

West Germany 2
Netherlands 1

7 July 1974 | Munich | Final

Of all the 68 goals Gerd Müller scored for West Germany, one in particular demonstrated all the qualities that made him the ultimate penalty-box predator. Fortunately, it was also the one that won the World Cup for his country. There were two minutes to go until half-time in the 1974 final against the Netherlands in Munich and the hosts had recovered from the shock of going behind in just the second minute to equalise. Rainer Bonhof hit a low cross towards the near post to where Müller had made a characteristically intelligent run. His first touch was unusually heavy, taking the ball behind him, but he retrieved the situation in an instant to spin and hit a shot across the goal into the opposite corner of the net. It was vintage Müller and, for all their talents, the Dutch could not recover. Müller had first announced himself on the world stage four years earlier when he won the Golden Boot in Mexico with 10 goals. One of those, an acrobatic close-range volley, completed West Germany's quarter-final comeback against England. It was also typical of his output, showing that unerring ability to be in the right place at the right time that is common to all great goalscorers. In his home tournament he was less prolific with four goals, but the fact that he hit winning strikes in what amounted to a semi-final against Poland and in the final showed his fondness for the great occasion.

RICHARD WHITEHEAD

Against a backdrop of his jubilant countrymen, Gerd Müller celebrates the goal that won the World Cup for West Germany.

Billy Bremner

Brazil 0 Scotland 0

18 June 1974 | Frankfurt
Group 2

FROM GEOFFREY GREEN, FOOTBALL CORRESPONDENT

Rivellino was booked 10 minutes before half-time for a dangerous tackle on Bremner from the rear and the longer the match raged the more these two repeated their running battle of Hampden Park a year ago when Brazil squeezed home 1-0. [...]

Bremner throughout the second half was a giant, a man clear cut against the horizon. Combative from first to last, his creativity suited the battle and, slipping like a hand into a glove, a perfect fit for the situation.

19 June

Pelé, the greatest Brazilian player, today acclaimed Scotland's captain, Bremner, as one of the outstanding stars of the World Cup finals. Twenty-four hours after Bremner had led the Scots to within inches of victory over Brazil, Pelé was still enthusing over the Scottish captain. "I really was most impressed by him," said Pelé, who is attending the finals at nearby Frankfurt in a private commercial capacity. "He is a great improviser and a very good leader of his team."

Billy Bremner and Brazil captain Piazza exchange pennants before their epic Group 2 battle in Frankfurt.

Billy Hamilton

Northern Ireland 2
Austria 2

1 July 1982 | Madrid
Second round, Group D

FROM STUART JONES, FOOTBALL CORRESPONDENT

Hamilton, the Irish hero, scored both goals. The first, on the half-hour was simple, direct and typically British. Armstrong, as strong and as willing as several oxen, ran past Pregesbauer and Obermayer, Austria's captain and sweeper, to the byline. There he crossed for Hamilton, Burnley's angular centre forward, to find a narrow gap with his head at the far post. It was not Ireland's first chance, nor was it by any means to be their last.

Earlier McCreery's drive had been collected and then dropped by Austria's goalkeeper, and before the break Armstrong presented himself with perhaps the clearest opportunity. Striding through the middle of Austria's defence, he found himself left with only Koncilia to beat. His shot was that of a tired man. [...]

When Hintermaier added the second with a ferocious free kick just as Brotherston joined the fray in place of Whiteside, the Irish, it was felt, must surely wither in the 100 degree heat. They should have been given much more credit. Running on limbs that must have been pumping automatically, they urged each other forward and were rewarded 15 minutes from the end. Armstrong's effort was deflected wide but Jimmy Nicholl refused to give up the chase, beating Koncilia to the loose ball.

He looped it over the retreating and scattered Austrian defence and there stood Hamilton, bronzed and patient, 10 yards out. With one deliberate nod of his blonde head he gave the Irish hope.

Billy Hamilton is congratulated by his teammates – his two goals against Austria gave Northern Ireland a chance of reaching the semi-finals.

Salvatore Schillaci

Italy 2 Czechoslovakia 0

19 June 1990 | Rome
Group A

FROM SIMON BARNES

The Italian manager, Azeglio Vicini, changed his strike force, leaving out Carnevale and Vialli, and starting instead with Schillaci and Baggio. And within nine minutes he was able to give himself the warmest possible congratulations.

Schillaci does not look the classical, blow-dried Italian boy; crew-cut and aggressive, he would be arrested on sight were he to step off the ferry at Cagliari. And he bagged, not a goal of classic beauty, but of classic appetite. Giannini walloped a volley at goal from outside the area, topped it and Schillaci plunged in to head the steeply rising ball into the net.

Italy 2 Uruguay 0

25 June 1990 | Rome
Second round

FROM SIMON BARNES

After half-time, Azeglio Vicini, the Italy coach, who had managed his options with great élan throughout the tournament, showed that he was as impatient as the crowd and all his players. He sent a third man into the attack, Serena, aged 30, from Inter Milan. At last a goal came, 20 minutes into the second half, and who but blazing-eyed Schillaci would score it? Serena's clever little ball put him through, and Schillaci, a man who, in a situation like this, has eyes only for goal, raced through and fairly walloped the ball into the net.

So great were the tensions, and so great the relief, that half the Italian side was in danger of arrest for indecent assault as they flung themselves on Schillaci to congratulate him.

A wide-eyed Schillaci is exultant after scoring in Italy's 1990 semi-final against Argentina. In a couple of weeks, he became a symbol of Italy's burning desire to win their home World Cup.

Gheorghe Hagi

Romania v Sweden

10 July 1994 | San Francisco
Quarter-final preview

FROM ROB HUGHES, FOOTBALL CORRESPONDENT

San Francisco may see an altogether more intriguing changing face of Europe when, tomorrow, Sweden meet Romania, who have never before reached the quarter-finals.

Indeed, Romania have turned up the temperature in terms of surprise and entertainment. Their playmaker, Gheorghe Hagi, a player known to the world shortly after his adolescence, is unquestionably thus far the man of the tournament. He scores with his left foot from astounding distances, from breathtaking angles. He conjures space out of nothing, a diminutive man built with the low centre of gravity of Maradona and Romário. He has the self-confidence that enables him to take the ball tight into the feet of opponents, to swivel, seemingly without looking, to direct snaking passes to his swift running team-mates, Ilie Dumitrescu and Florin Raducioiu.

Tomorrow, the staring eyes of Thomas Ravelli, Sweden's experienced goalkeeper, must be constantly alert.

Gheorghe Hagi, the arch creator, is thrilled after his pass creates a goal for Ilie Dumitrescue in Romania's second-round win over Argentina.

Paul McGrath

Ireland 1 Italy 0

18 June 1994 | New Jersey
Group E

FROM HUGH MCILVANNEY

That roar had plenty of heroes to salute on a day when Ireland did not have a failure, but none left more thrilling images to shimmer in the memory than Paul McGrath. This 34-year-old defender, whose life has been plagued with troubles, many of his own making, whose very presence on the field is a small miracle given the ravaged state of his knees, gave an epic performance. Alongside him Phil Babb, who was having his first competitive match for the Republic but looked as if it were his 50th, was an ideal ally.

There are 11 years between them but in terms of composure they behaved like twins.

McGrath's mastery was perfectly represented by a moment in the second half when the ball came at him awkwardly with Italian forwards closing in and he left us convinced that the only practical option was the elaborate back-heeled clearance with which he saved his team yet again. It was enough to give every other team in the World Cup an inferiority complex.

Paul McGrath produced a performance of breathtaking authority to subdue Roberto Baggio and the rest of Italy's stellar forward line.

Romário

Brazil 2 Russia 0

20 June 1994 | San Francisco
Group B

FROM SIMON BARNES

"I am prepared to die for the glory of Brazilian football," Romário said before the match, which is the sort of thing that any Brazilian superstar is expected to say. Saying it is easy enough. The problem is bearing the weight of all their country's and the world's expectations; bearing the weight of all that tonnage of pure gold.

This has tended, too often in the recent past, to bring out not joy but worry. Increasingly, Brazilians have had to wear an ever more gaudy carnival mask to hide the ever-growing national angst. [...]

The players are simply not familiar enough with each other's cast of mind – and their style leaves no margin for error. Too much of what they tried requires both genius and consistency from Romário. He is not quite capable of the one and seldom even strives for the other.

In the next week, he must find a new dimension within himself. To sum up, this version of Brazil has everything it needs in footballing terms – except for cohesion and goals.

Flag day: Romário shows his true colours to the crowd in San Francisco after Brazil's second-round win over the United States.

David Villa

Spain 1 Paraguay 0

3 July 2010 | Johannesburg
Quarter-final

FROM MATT HUGHES,
DEPUTY FOOTBALL CORRESPONDENT

For such a multitalented team, Spain appear awfully reliant on one individual. David Villa has scored five of his side's six goals as the European champions have scrapped their way to the last four of the World Cup for the first time since 1950, showing the patience to keep faith with their passing principles, but just as importantly demonstrating the resilience of serial winners.

Those at the FA charged with arresting the crisis in English player development should take a look at Villa, who has emerged as a template for the complete footballer after scoring the winner against Paraguay. The player's superlative form represents a triumph for poise over power, inspiration over perspiration and technique over tenacity, qualities sadly lacking in the English game, making the failure of any Premier League club to sign Villa all the more mysterious.

Villa's tally of 43 goals in 63 matches for Spain catches the eye, but he offers so much more. In five games in South Africa, the Barcelona striker has played in three different positions, showing a flexibility and willingness unheard of in England to subsume personal ambitions to those of the team. Villa is equally comfortable operating as a spearhead, second striker or even out wide, although given Fernando Torres's poor form, Vicente Del Bosque, the coach, is keen for him to operate as close to goal as possible.

With a typically assured finish, David Villa scores Spain's late winner in their quarter-final victory over Paraguay.

Cristiano Ronaldo

Portugal 3 Spain 3
15 June 2018 | Sochi | Group B

FROM OLIVER KAY, CHIEF FOOTBALL CORRESPONDENT

On an extraordinary night in Sochi, in one of the most thrilling World Cup matches in many years, Cristiano Ronaldo refused to allow Spain's redemption story to overshadow his own. With a spectacular hat-trick, culminating in a free kick to level the scores with two minutes remaining, the irrepressible Portugal captain made the most resounding statement of intent, almost single-handedly denying Spain the victory they craved at the end of a torrid week.

In keeping with a chaotic build-up, the action was non-stop. There was controversy over refereeing decisions, a terrible mistake by David De Gea, a terrific Spain comeback inspired by the contrasting figures of Andres Iniesta and Diego Costa, and a spectacular goal from Nacho to put them 3-2 up. Ultimately, though, it kept coming back to Ronaldo, who produced one of the greatest performances of his international career.

Some still argue that Ronaldo has never really done it for his country. Really? He was not as integral to their European Championship success two years ago as might have been imagined, but these were his 82nd, 83rd and 84th goals in 151 appearances for Portugal, taking him level with Ferenc Puskas, the great Hungarian, in second place in the all-time international goalscoring charts behind the Iranian striker Ali Daei. Last night he became the first player to score in eight leading international tournaments and only the fourth to score at four World Cups. He is astonishing.

Spain's Sergio Busquets struggles to keep up with a rampant Ronaldo during Portugal's thrilling 3-3 draw with Spain in Sochi.

Index

Acknowledgements

A number of people were instrumental in bringing this book to fruition and deserve my grateful thanks. At HarperCollins, Jethro Lennox and Harley Griffiths shaped the direction of the book while Robin Scrimgeour proved to a superb project manager, making several important suggestions about the presentation of the material, and Kevin Robbins designed an excellent cover. Tim Hallissey, former Head of Sport at The Times, was, as always, an enormously helpful sounding board. When facts needed to be checked and my memory needed jogging Bill Edgar, the paper's peerless numbers man, was invaluable. I'd also like to thank Chief Football Writer Henry Winter for his foreword. The wonderful team at the News UK archive were incredibly helpful and always quick off the mark, including Nick Mayes, Michael-John Jennings, Sue De Friend and Chris Ball. I would also like to thank Robin Ashton, Ian Brunskill and David Luxton.

Photo credits

Cover (front) Daniel Motz/Press Association Images;
Cover (back) Colorsport/Shutterstock;
P4-5 Neil Libbert Fred Harris / Times Newspapers;
P10-11 REUTERS / Alamy Stock Photo;
P12-13 Popperfoto / Getty Images;
P14-15 Horace TOnge / Times Newspapers;
P17 IBL/Shutterstock;
P18 John Alex Maguire/Shutterstock;
P20-21 Central Press / Getty Images;
P23 Rolls Press/Popperfoto / Getty Images;
P25 Rolls Press/Popperfoto / Getty Images;
P26-27 Trinity Mirror / Mirrorpix / Alamy Stock Photo;
P28 Inpho Photography / Getty Images;
P31 REUTERS / Alamy Stock Photo;
P32 Tim Sharp/AP/Shutterstock;
P34-35 Bob Thomas / Getty Images;
P37 REUTERS / Alamy Stock Photo;
P38-39 PA Images / Alamy Stock Photo;
P40-41 Sipa/Shutterstock;
P42 Javier Etxezarreta/EPA-EFE/Shutterstock;
P44-45 Colorsport/Shutterstock;
P47 ullstein bild Dtl. / Getty Images;
p48-49 TT News Agency / Alamy Stock Photo;
P51 Popperfoto /Getty Images;
P52-53 Werner Otto / Alamy Stock Photo;
P54-55 PA Images / Alamy Stock Photo;
P56-57 Luca Bruno/AP/Shutterstock;
P58-59 Back Page Images/Shutterstock;
P60-61 Chema Moya/EPA/Shutterstock;
P62-63 Sipa/Shutterstock;
P64 AP/Shutterstock;
P66-67 Action Plus Sports Images / Alamy Stock Photo;
P68-69 Imago/BPI/Shutterstock;
P70 Colorsport/Shutterstock;
P73 (top) David Cannon / Getty Images;
(bottom) David Cannon / Getty Images;
P74 Henri Szwarc / Getty Images;
P77 Dusan Vranic/AP/Shutterstock;
P78 Credit: Abaca Press / Alamy Stock Photo;
P80-81 Ben Queenborough/BPI/Shutterstock;
P82-83 Keystone / Getty Images;

P85 Action Plus Sports Images / Alamy Stock Photo;
P86-87 Neil Leifer / Getty Images;
P88-89 AP/Shutterstock;
P90 (top) Trinity Mirror / Mirrorpix / Alamy Stock Photo;
(bottom) Paul Popper/Popperfoto / Getty Images;
P92-93 Ben Radford / Getty Images;
P94-95 Marc Aspland
P96-97 Colorsport/Shutterstock;
P99 Colorsport/Shutterstock;
P100-101 Achim Scheidemann/EPA/Shutterstock;
P102-103 Bernat Armangue/AP/Shutterstock;
P104-105 Martin Meissner/AP/Shutterstock;
P106-107 Wang Lili/Shutterstock;
P109 Seb Wells/Pixathlon/Sipa/Shutterstock;
P111 Hollandse Hoogte/Shutterstock;
P112-113 Dave Shopland/BPI/Shutterstock;
P114-115 Popperfoto / Getty Images,
P116-117 Haynes Archive/Popperfoto / Getty Images;
P118-119 Trinity Mirror / Mirrorpix / Alamy Stock Photo;
P120 Neil Libbert Fred Harris / Times Newspapers;
P122 Neil Libbert Fred Harris / Times Newspapers;
P123 Neil Libbert Fred Harris / Times Newspapers;
P125 Popperfoto / Getty Images;
P126 Paul Popper/Popperfoto / Getty Images;
P128-129 Paul Popper/Popperfoto / Getty Images;
P130-131 Trinity Mirror / Mirrorpix / Alamy Stock Photo;
P133 Jean-Yves Ruszniewski / Getty Images;
P134-135 Kieran Galvin/Shutterstock;
P137 PA Images / Alamy Stock Photo;
P138 Dave Shopland/BPI/Shutterstock;
P140-141 Amy Sancetta/AP/Shutterstock;
P142-143 Popperfoto / Getty Images;
P144 dpa picture alliance / Alamy Stock Photo;
P147 PA Images / Alamy Stock Photo;
P148-149 Trinity Mirror / Mirrorpix / Alamy Stock Photo;
P151 REUTERS / Alamy Stock Photo;
P152 REUTERS / Alamy Stock Photo;

P155 Amy Sancetta/AP/Shutterstock;
P156 Thanassis Stavrakis/AP/Shutterstock;
P158-159 Bob Thomas / Getty Images;
P160 PAGES Francois / Getty Images;
P162-163 Popperfoto / Getty Images;
P164 ITV/Shutterstock;
P166-167 Trinity Mirror / Mirrorpix / Alamy Stock Photo;
P169 AP/Shutterstock;
P170-171 Imago/Shutterstock;
P172 Bob Thomas / Getty Images;
P174-175 Getty Images;
P176 INTERFOTO / Alamy Stock Photo;
P179 (top) Marc Aspland / Times Newspapers, (bottom) Marc Aspland / Times Newspapers;
P180 Yuri Kochetkov/EPA/Shutterstock;
P182-183 Alessandra Tarantino/AP/Shutterstock;
P184-185 Ricardo Mazalan/AP/Shutterstock;
P186-187 OMAR TORRES / Getty Images;
P188 Colorsport/Shutterstock;
P191 Colorsport/Shutterstock;
P192-193 Aflo Co. Ltd. / Alamy Stock Photo;
P194-195 Shutterstock;
P196-197 Marc Aspland / Times Newspapers;
P199 Marc Aspland / Times Newspapers;
P200-201 Roland Weihrauch/EPA/Shutterstock;
P203 Michael Zemanek/BPI/Shutterstock;
P204-205 PA Images / Alamy Stock Photo;
P206 Popperfoto / Getty Images;
P207 Trinity Mirror / Mirrorpix / Alamy Stock Photo;
P208 Fred Shepherd / Times Newspapers.
P209 Alfred Harris / Times Newspapers;
P210-211 Colorsport/Shutterstock;
P212 PA Images / Alamy Stock Photo;
P213 PA Images / Alamy Stock Photo;
P215 DANIEL GARCIA / Getty Images;
P216 Douglas C Pizac/AP/Shutterstock;
P217 PA Images / Alamy Stock Photo;
P218 Stephen Dunn / Getty Images;
P219 Shutterstock;
P220-221 Michael Zemanek/BPI/Shutterstock

Photo captions

Page 10-11
South Africa fans tune up their vuvuzelas before the host nation's opening match against Mexico at Johannesburg in 2010.

Page 44-45
Against the backdrop of an Aztec stadium throbbing with expectation, the sublime Brazil team of 1970 wait to take on Italy in the final.

Page 62-63
Chaos reigns as Argentina attempt a lap of the Aztec stadium after their 3-2 victory over West Germany in the 1986 final. But there is no doubt about the architect of their triumph – No.10 Diego Maradona.

Page 80-81
Colombia's James Rodríguez watches the flight of his perfectly struck volley as it makes its way towards the top corner of the Uruguay net in 2014.

Page 114-115
Let battle commence: the teams emerge from the tunnel in Guadalajara for one of the epic battles in World Cup history – Brazil v England in 1970.

Page 140-141
The South Korea players celebrate their second-round win over Italy in front of a disbelieving home crowd in Daejeon in 2002.

Page 158-159
On hand to score: Diego Maradona has just used his hand to flick the ball over England goalkeeper Peter Shilton to give Argentina the lead in the 1986 quarter-final. Did he dare to hope he would get away with it?

Page 186-187
A disconsolate Italy striker Roberto Baggio realises his missed penalty in the 1994 final shoot-out has just handed the World Cup to Brazil.

Page 204-205
Eusébio is not given time even to leave the field at Goodison Park before an enterprising journalist asks him about his four goals for Portugal against North Korea in 1966.

Writers featured

Simon Barnes, Rick Broadbent, George Caulkin, Barry Davies, Matt Dickinson (Football Correspondent, 2000-2007), Roddy Forsyth, Norman Fox (Football Correspondent, 1976-1981), Tom German, Brian Glanville (Sunday Times Football Correspondent, 1958-1992), Geoffrey Green (Football Correspondent, 1946-1976), Ian Hawkey, Paul Hirst, Oliver Holt (Football Correspondent, 1997-2000), Matt Hughes, Rob Hughes (Football Correspondent, 1993-1997), Stuart Jones (Football Correspondent, 1981-1993), Paul Joyce, Oliver Kay (Football Correspondent, 2009-2019), Kevin McCarra, Hugh McIlvanney (The Sunday Times), David Miller, Alyson Rudd, Gerald Sinstadt, Rory Smith, Matthew Syed, Graham Taylor, Clive White, Henry Winter (Chief Football Writer, 2015-).